Rosie

*Selected Works
by Rosemary Richmond*

*For Phyllis --
Birthday, 1995
love from Jackie
(and all of us)*

ROSEHILL PRESS
Springfield, Illinois

Publication of this work was supported in part by a grant from the Springfield Area Arts Council and by contributions from friends of Rosemary Richmond.

ROSEHILL PRESS EDITION

Copyright © 1995 by Brainchild Writers of Springfield
All rights reserved.

Cover photo:
Linda Smogor

Inside photo:
Ginny Lee of Springfield, Illinois

Printer:
United Graphics Inc. of Mattoon, Illinois

Publisher:
Rosehill Press
545 South Feldkamp Avenue
Springfield, Illinois 62704

ISBN 0-9646037-2-1

Manufactured in the United States of America
on recycled paper using soy inks.

To Rosemary Richmond, from her friends

Three flights up
painted green with spaces
showing below the ground
and hard cement like Aunt
Lot's in Peoria only white and
Brother laughing. But there's
no fear like then.

At the top not even out of
breath I swing open the
wood gate and enter the
porch — flowered benches and
tables and a wicker couch
full of softness, inviting
like Rosie who greets me,
"Hello, Sweetheart" with
a hug — her ampleness less
from without than within.

"Home" for an evening
with friends, with sisters
I never had, with loving critics
who say, "shut up, read it,"
and Rosie directs with a velvet
hand her stage furnished with
eclectic collections from
eclectic friends.

Beer and popcorn — no wine and
bread. Ours is a communion
that is disjointed but never
ends. And if there's a heaven
where feminist writers blend their
voices in ethereal chorus it
must be three flights up,
painted green with safe open
spaces in between.

Bonnie Madison

Contents

Acknowledgements ... 7
Foreword ... 9
Introduction ... 14

Stories

    Socks and Earrings ... 19
    Don't Get Me Wrong ... 29
    Triple-Word Sting ... 32
    Flag Day ... 37
    The Fourth of July ... 41
    Saab Story ... 44
    Angel ... 47
    Hair Trigger ... 51
    Joanne Throws a Party ... 54
    Christmas Cake ... 59
    Love to Larry ... 67
    The Screening Committee ... 69
    Death and Jane ... 73
    The Laundromat ... 79
    Two Whole Nutmegs ... 85
    Rage ... 89
    Peace in the Valley ... 93
    Kitty ... 96
    Chapel of Love ... 101

Poems

    Bad Blood ... 107
    Graduate Assistant's Lament ... 108
    So What? ... 109
    Untitled (Brainchild) ... 110
    Time ... 110
    Pause in Between ... 110

Feminists Need Cents ... 111
Filing ... 111
No Piecemeal Deal ... 111
A Good Old Time ... 112
Untitled (But she thought) ... 112
On the Verge Of ... 113
Recipe ... 113
Untitled (My family thinks I'm mad) ... 114
Marking Time ... 115
Untitled (My mother dresses me) ... 115
Untitled (My child is gone) ... 115
Cracked Glass ... 116
Dreams (I dream of roller coasters)... 116
Dope Man ... 117
Untitled (The train dances along) ... 117
Sanfran, Union Square ... 118
Untitled (I've taken all the insults) ... 119
Silhouette ... 119
Rain ... 120
Dreams (We lie sleeping) ... 120
Spring Tune-up ... 121
First Night ... 121
Vachel's Place ... 122

Essays

A Day in the Life ... 125
If I Had Money ... 129
Stepmothers ... 131
Nastiness Turned Simple-minded ... 133
A Very Fishy Story ... 135
Sylvia Beach Hotel ... 137
How to Get Along Without a Car ... 141
The Artful Punster ... 144
Hammons Comes Home ... 149

Novel Excerpts

Walking Stories ... 161
Fifth Position (No Compromising Positions) ... 166
Fifth Position (Excerpt) ... 171

About the Author ... 179
To Rosie ... 180

Acknowledgements

When Rosemary Richmond died on March 1, 1994, she left behind dozens of manuscripts, many of them — too many of them — unpublished. Her women's writing collective, Brainchild Writers of Springfield, decided an anthology of selected works would be a fitting tribute to a woman who had nurtured so many in the Springfield, Illinois, writing community. Of course, many hands make light work, and Brainchild owes a debt of gratitude to the dozens of individuals who helped with this project.

First, we would like to thank Rosie Richmond's daughter Stacia Stinnett for lending us photos, allowing us access to original manuscripts and granting us permission to publish the work you will read in this book.

We'd like to express our appreciation to Rosie's friends Carol Corgan and Polly Poskin from the Illinois Coalition Against Sexual Assault. They went through Rosie's files and collected every manuscript or fragment they could find, however unfinished, and copied them all (at least two full boxes) for Brainchild.

A seven-member Rosie Richmond Anthology Committee then spent several months of additional sorting while seeking consensus on what should go in the book. Some stories were universal favorites, while others did not appear to be quite finished. This left the selection committee with some tough decisions. Committee members included Becky Bradway, Gael Carnes, Debi Edmund, Jacqueline Jackson, Kate Kanaley Miller, Peg Knoepfle and Bonnie Madison.

Gael Carnes and her husband John spent several hours scanning stories and poems onto computer diskettes, thus saving dozens of typesetting hours. Rosehill Press owners Debi Edmund and Peter Ellertsen then took over the job of typesetting, editing, design, working with the printer, fund-raising and publicity for the book.

Several of the stories in this anthology were originally

published in other places. We would like to acknowledge those sources. Appearing in the *Alchemist Review* were "Socks and Earrings," "Triple Word Sting," "Joanne Throws a Party," "The Screening Committee," "The Laundromat," "Two Whole Nutmegs," "Graduate Assistant's Lament," "Stepmothers" and a *Fifth Position* excerpt. Appearing in *Writers' Bar-B-Q* were "Flag Day," "The Fourth of July," "Saab Story" and "Rage." Appearing in anthologies published by Brainchild Writers of Springfield were "Angel," "Christmas Cake," "Peace in the Valley" and *Walking Stories*. "The Artful Punster" originally appeared in *Illinois Times*. We also are grateful to all the people who shared the "Rosie stories" included in the anthology's introduction.

Without the help of a generous grant from the Springfield Area Arts Council, and the help of good friends who made special contributions above the price of a book purchase, *Rosie: Selected Works by Rosemary Richmond* could not have been published. We thank the following sponsors for their generosity:

Ricardo M. Amézquita
G.M.A.
Sandra Bartholmey
Gael Carnes
Carol Corgan
L.J. "Lucky" Cuoco
Lynda Dautenhahn
Janice DiGirolamo
Judith Everson
David Everson
Jane Fee
Ronda Fraser
Lee Gaeding
Bonnie Hermann-Cook
Barbara Hildebrand
Kathy Howell
Ron Howell
Illinois Times
John Knoepfle
Peg Knoepfle
Carolyn Cochran Kopel
Heidi Kon
Gloria J. Leitschuh
Donna Lennon
Michael Lennon
Naomi B. Lynn
Bonnie Madison
P.J. Burtle-McCredie
Roger E. McCredie
Lee Nickelson
Victor Pearn
Polly Poskin
Sharon Poskin
Milli Quam
Kathleen Quinn
Richard D. Raymond
Donna Rich-Murdock
Dr. Rose Marie Roach
Lynette Seator
Bob Sipe
Debra Nickelson Smith
J. Christopher Smith
Liesl G. Smith
Martha Whitaker-McGil
Kathy Wood
An "Angel Gift"

All these people played a vital role in getting Rosie's work where it belongs — into the hands of the public.

Foreword

It was told to me concerning Rosie that she never had much in the way of material possessions but that she counted her wealth in friends; in that respect, she was very rich indeed.
— *Rabbi Barry A. Marks, Temple Israel*

Whether at parties, business gatherings, arts festivals or political rallies, you could hear some variation on the following conversation:

"Rosemary Richmond. You know — Rosie?"

"Oh yeah. I know who *she* is."

Everyone in Springfield, Illinois, it seems, knew Rosemary Richmond. Everyone who knew her, it seems, has a "Rosie story" to tell.

"Hell," says Springfield playwright and fiction writer Gary Smith. "She's such a legend."

Rosemary Richmond, a vital member of the Springfield arts and academic communities, died of cancer on March 1, 1994. She was 49.

Rosie began her writing career while attending Sangamon State University as a "nontraditional" student. "I knew Rosie ... from her entrance into Sangamon State back in the 1970s," says English professor Judy Everson. "She struck me then as exactly the kind of student our university had been created to serve — the place-bound adult returning to higher education after a stop-out for marriage and children. Rosie was bright, eager, intellectually inquisitive. It was a joy to watch her respond to books, ideas, experiences, opportunities."

Rosie went on to be widely published locally — *Illinois Times*, the *Alchemist Review*, *Writers' Bar-B-Q*, *Two-Way Mirrors*, *XX Chromosome Chronicle* and anthologies produced by Brainchild

Writers of Springfield. She performed dozens of readings and won her share of awards. "I took such pride in her developing artistic voice," says Judy Everson, "not just in what she wrote, but in how she read her work: skillfully, soulfully."

"She was writing about things we all had experienced but had never dared talk about," says Peg Knoepfle, with Rosie a founding member of Brainchild. "God it was fun to hear these stories, to read them. The emotions that seared our souls or shamed our sense of propriety and good morals, the conflicts that had no solution, the possibilities that scared the hell out of us were transformed in Rosie's stories into hilarious lamenting ruminations and odd but completely plausible events — and rounded off with Rosie Richmond one-liners. Rowdy, rambunctious and right on the mark."

Rosie's apartment on South Grand Avenue became a home away from home for members of Brainchild, a women's writing collective. "I remember walking in the door of her apartment and seeing her there, popping corn, tossing a 'hiya, honey' over her shoulder," says Brainchild "sister" Gael Carnes. "I think of her sitting in a room full of candles, her feet tucked under her while she focuses on me, listening to what I have to say or read with flattering intensity."

Rena Brannan, a Brainchild sister now living in California, describes the magic of meetings at Rosie's: "Coke with a few ice cubes. Popcorn in a big green bowl. Oil hanging in the air. So many words. So many words. I sat at that table round and plump from the power of some of the greatest writers on this planet. More admirable than Dorothy Parker's roundtable."

Rena remembers, at age 19, "climbing those stairs to Rosie's ... shaking, my nerve, my one last nerve, almost lost, looking through her back door, looking into what would become my future ball. I mean ball, the grandest times. Ballroom writing. Ballroom talking. The most significant part of my growing into my work as an artist, as a writer, happened in that apartment."

"There was no one who even came close to her apt way of looking at everyday life and finding some value in the struggle," says Gael. "She could make me laugh at things that hurt the most, or feel saddened by the simple act of shopping for clothes."

It was very important to Rosie that her stories be funny. It was her standard of quality, says Peg. "It took longer than it should have to recognize that these little stories we all loved so much and felt so easy with were dealing with big subjects. Rosie's stories go to the heart of things. She was funny because she was never trivial. You look at what she wrote about. The big-time subjects.

The hard subjects. The ones we have trouble talking about, let alone putting on paper. She covered them all."

Besides her Brainchild sisters, Rosie nurtured other writers and artists in the community at every opportunity. "She was always eager to share constructive criticism and advice with other writers," says *Illinois Times* editor Bill Furry. Her public access television show *Works in Progress*, which she and co-producer Peg Knoepfle hosted for several years, profiled area artists and their ongoing creative projects.

"Rosie did indeed fall in love with her subjects," wrote artist Mauri Formigoni, assistant professor in SSU's visual arts program, in a letter to *Illinois Times*. "Watching the TV series she produced with Peg Knoepfle — interviewing the artists and writers, taking in their whole gig, their stuff, their energy — I saw how much she rejoiced in the art and the life which surrounds it."

But Rosie's gift for the written word was not the only reason people found her so memorable.

Friends recall how nurtured and encouraged and understood they felt just being in Rosie's presence — the broad grin and devilish gleam in her eyes as she delivered one of her trademark hilarious observations. "Rosie had the gift to touch others with her spirit," says Judi O'Brien Anderson, professor of English at Springfield College in Illinois. "When she welcomed you, you felt welcomed."

Friends say Rosie was always the one reaching out, telling other people how great *they* were. "You know ... I've been in business almost 15 years," says Lee Gaeding, owner of PRO TYPE, a Springfield typesetting company. "I've had hundreds of customers. But Rosie is the only one I could count on, when she would see the finished product, to say, 'Oh, how wonderful!'"

Rosie's annual Christmas parties attained legendary status in Springfield. People you wouldn't expect to find in the same room stood shoulder to shoulder in her apartment, singing Christmas carols in the living room, reciting poetry in the kitchen.

"Her Christmas parties were some of the most enjoyable I have ever attended," says Gael Carnes. "And not just because of the secret punch in the punch, but because of the eclectic group of people who genuinely cared for Rosie and who would gather together in one small apartment. The conversation was always interesting, the views varied."

Rosie once joked that she preferred to think of the unemployment checks she received for a short time as "a grant from the National Endowment for the Arts" to pursue fiction writing full-time. But even though Rosie never realized her dream of making a living at writing fiction, she worked her writing skills and her feminist politics into many of the paying jobs she held.

For several years she wrote newsletters, brochures and training materials for such organizations as the Illinois Coalition Against Sexual Assault, the Illinois Coalition Against Domestic Violence and the Springfield Rape Information and Counseling Service. She also conducted training for volunteers and board members of these organizations.

"Rosie sparkled with possibility," says Carol Corgan, a friend who works at the Illinois Coalition Against Sexual Assault. "Whether we were gossiping, telling our dreams, planning a potluck or musing over some improbable future project, magic and the promise of joy were always right there. She could imagine anything. ... Her writing is a reminder of these gifts."

Even when she worked in the basement of a bank or sold insurance to pay the rent, she managed to put a humorous spin on things. Maurice "Dewey" DeWimille, an old friend who worked with Rosie during her days at a Springfield bank, recalls, "I was always a big grouch — never smiling. She and another friend gave me a wire clothes hanger to put in my mouth in order to create a smile."

Says Judy Everson: "She had the ability to take what she needed from a variety of different sources, so that she had friends from many backgrounds, but she remained her own person, independent and eclectic in her outlook."

It was this exuberance, empathy and non-stop sense of humor — qualities Rosie possessed in abundance — that made her stand out in the minds of so many who knew her.

Rabbi Barry Marks, in his eulogy delivered March 3, 1994, touched on another quality of Rosie's:

> Judaism's tradition has been called a down-to-earth mysticism. We seek God's presence, not by distancing ourselves from daily life, not in some far-off locale or esoteric experience, but rather within the realm of the everyday — through eating, drinking, celebration and companionship, and through appreciating the wonders and beauties of Creation. My acquaintance with Rosie leads me to believe that she possessed such a pragmatic and down-to-earth temperament. She described herself and her circle of friends as being 'rowdy,' but I believe that along with the rowdiness, there was a serious and profound spirituality.

Rosie was a great lover of angels. Indeed, "Angel" was one of her nicknames. Rabbi Marks noted, "The word for angel in Hebrew, *malach*, means 'messenger.' Through her artistry, Rosie created a song of praise to life and its potential."

The Sunday after Rosie died, more than 300 people gathered at the old St. Nicholas Hotel for a two-hour-long tribute, "A Celebration of Rosie's Life." We celebrated a woman who inspired us with her strength in living the kind of life she wanted to live, and not a life that might have been easier but less authentic. We celebrated Rosie as one of those rare people who followed her own creative flame, nurtured and fed it and was true to it even through the most difficult times.

A year later, Brainchild members talk of how they still (almost) expect Rosie to breeze in the door at any minute, calling out her extravagant greetings and passing around a bowl of popcorn.

"I miss Rosie," says Brainchild's Gael Carnes. "I miss talking 'Rosie talk' and seeing that special spin that only she could give. I miss her in the empty rooms I walk. I miss turning to her and receiving her little hugs. I don't hug others easily. ... We always talk around the word 'love,' especially with friends. I miss her. I look up to her apartment. For me, there will always be an empty room where Rosie once lived. Hopefully, she will haunt me forever."

Shortly before her death, longtime friend and former Brainchild member Jessica Billings wrote to Rosie, "You are such a powerful woman. We are drawn to your power. And to your sweet, fierce beauty. Do you know that, Rosie? Do you know your power? Do you know your beauty? Do you know the love you have inspired?"

Writer. Feminist. Rabble-rouser. Friend. Ally. Healer. Angel. Solid gold. Through wit and pen and person, Rosie gave us herself, her unforgettable personhood. She was and is loved, admired, envied, cherished, emulated, respected and, most of all, appreciated.

Debi Sue Edmund

Debi Sue Edmund is co-owner, with her husband Peter Ellertsen, of Rosehill Press. She is a member of Brainchild Writers of Springfield and has been a journalist for the past 15 years. Her short stories and articles have appeared in local, regional and national publications.

Introduction

Knowing Rosie Richmond's fiction and also having known Rosie, it can be difficult to separate the woman from her work. Rosie's personality was partly fiction and Rosie's fiction was largely Rosie and Rosie was a force, in writing and in life. She was in your face, in a nice way. She was an original. She was honest. She was vulnerable. These words apply to both Rosie, the sensual feminist, and Rosie's writing, full of sensuality, politics, humor and openness.

Rosie's work takes risks that many writers' fiction does not: risks of honesty in showing heterosexual sexuality, sex roles, family and poverty. That Rosie's work stayed mostly within her own community during her lifetime reflects a problem that was also her greatest strength: her vulnerability. Rosie just wouldn't send the stuff out — her skin wasn't thick enough to handle the reams of rejection slips that published writers learn to put up with. Every rejection was a personal one, just as every one of her stories was personal and from the heart. She was insecure about her writing, as she was about herself — she was never sure it or she was good enough. This insecurity made her charming, modest and generous as a person. But it is largely this that kept her writing from finding the wide audience it deserves. Perhaps a loyalty to her town and her friends was also at work — while she talked and dreamed of leaving Springfield, she never did.

When I met Rosie, I was in my early 20s. Rosie's own modesty may have kept many young and not-so-young writers from fully realizing what effect her willingness to tackle tough and painful subjects had on their work. What it did was free us. Her stories and novels reflected daring, a wild spirit, a willingness to talk frankly about sex and men, an affinity for female friendships and a raucous sense of humor that had an immeasurable impact on me and others. In her writing, Rosie went deep and she came up smiling — or, at least, with a few good jokes. Moxie, an old-fashioned word, comes to mind — or maybe guts is better. Rosie could go after the emotional core of herself and others and come up hurt, brave and never self-pitying.

This book contains much of Rosie's best completed work. Her novel *Fifth Position*, perhaps the earliest of her writing included here, is among her nerviest stuff. A look at post-60s sexual and political female angst, it is a hoot of a book that in its entirety deserves a wide readership. Rosie was a beloved local essayist and certainly also whipped off some clever and funny poems, but for me her best work is her short stories. Going after the core of female longing — for love, for companionship, for commitment, for a damn fun time — are stories like "Flag Day," "Triple Word Sting," "The Screening Committee" and "Don't Get Me Wrong." Romantically about that ideal guy who could maybe do it up good on a hot day and then manage to be nice and carry on an artsy conversation, Rosie literally bared her dreams. They are fantasies juxtaposed with the ever-underlying tension that things between men and women are mostly not quite what we wish them to be.

Rosie also wrote of family: her disjointed, poor, Jewish, matriarchal family of origin and her children, often her daughter. These stories — "Christmas Cake," "Rage," "Joanne Throws a Party" — relate, along with closeness, a sad frustration at the inability of the family to come together in the socially-expected normal family way. Again, there is tension between what we want and hope for and try to make happen, and what actually does happen: dissension, discomfort and anger. What Rosie does in her relationship stories is expose the vulnerabilities all of us experience when it comes to loving others — men and women, moms and kids.

Rosie did another type of writing, perhaps best exemplified by "Walking Stories," about a woman on her own viewing the world with a quizzical eye. Our main character is basically walking along, minding her own business, when she gets hit upside the head with some oddity of existence. This might be having a bag lady in her car, or finding her groceries stolen, or overhearing a weird conversation. These seemingly small events carry a charming profundity about daily life: Isn't this strange, Rosie (or Ellen, or whoever) seems to say. Aren't we all incredibly strange, pathetic people, and why does this keep happening to me, and isn't it all rather funny? Aren't I a shlub (to leave my groceries in the unlocked car, to be out walking too far, to be daydreaming), and aren't you all shlubs too and aren't we all in this together? Ha! That these pieces are among her most popular is a testament to Rosie's ability to link us in our own inadequate humanness.

The look at daily routines and personal quirks might make Rosie's stories seem simple. Don't be deceived. All of Rosie's work is based in a certain sorrow and confusion about a world beyond the control of her characters. This becomes more apparent in her later stories, such as "Hair Trigger" and "Love to Larry," in which it is clear that perhaps the big dreams will not come to be and there is hereditary weight that cannot be cast away. That her characters respond to their struggles with humor, strength, tenacity, stubbornness and a philosophical determination to move on through it might lead us to think it's all easy. But transcending poverty and childhood pain and struggling with single parenthood and romantic angst is never easy, in life or in fiction. It's a testament to Rosie that she gets us laughing so hard that sometimes we forget what's really going on in there.

Rosie wrote through the '70s, '80s and early '90s — always forward and honest and committed to her beliefs about the freedoms women should have. Now, in 1995, there are Riot Girls — young feminists taking over music and walking the university halls. Well, Rosie was a riot and a riot girl before it was cool. Any current or potential high-spirited, open-minded, open-hearted riot girl or boy of any age should get their hands on this book and read it cover to cover. It transcends Springfield. It should be in New York, California, Aruba and anywhere else that Rosie ever wanted to live.

Becky Bradway

Becky Bradway, fiction writer and an editor of Writers' Bar-B-Q, *has published many stories. Her work will appear in* Mondo Barbie 2 *(St. Martin's) and* Crescent Review, *and was most recently published in* Green Mountain Review, Beloit Fiction Journal *and* Eating Our Hearts Out: Women and Food *(Crossing Press).*

Stories

Socks and Earrings

"This doesn't fit," Ellen tells the salesclerk. "Can you bring in a larger size? Maybe a 16?"

She is aware that the clerk has put her in the dressing room with the window. She knows what is behind the Laura Ashley curtains that cover the glass pane. She hopes she will not look.

"I'm not sure we have that suit in a 16. Is there something else you would like to try? We have a Ralph Lauren taupe wool suit that's very nice."

"Yes," Ellen says. "Bring that." She stands in the dressing room, tries to force the size-14 skirt on her overweight body. She stares at her bulges, wonders why she has let herself go. Her hair is a mixture of colors: red, brown, gray, blonde. The style is frizzy from the permanent which she just got, but which she doesn't like. Her hair and stomach, she thinks — if only she could remedy those two problems.

The salesclerk knocks lightly. "Here's the Lauren. I do hope you have better luck with this. It's just a lovely color for winter. You can wear anything with it."

"Like what?" Ellen asks. She wants specifics. She only has two blouses that will button in her closet. They are blue and hot pink. Will those colors go with taupe?

"Anything. You can wear anything with taupe. It goes with everything."

"You know," Ellen says, "my values have changed since I've gained weight. I used to be very concerned with what I wore. It had to look just right. But lately, I don't care what I wear. I'll buy anything that fits. But nothing does."

There is no response. Ellen begins to talk to herself. Maybe I should try a large sweater, she says to her image in the mirror. Something to hide fat.

She checks the size again to make sure it is a 16. She slips the skirt over her head; it slides over her hips, but it will not button. Ellen stares into the mirror again, resigned, frustrated, unhappy and bored. Bored with trying on clothes that won't fit, bored with worrying about weight, bored with the idea of going to a fat group where people discuss potatoes, desserts, calories, waistline sizes, pounds registered on a scale, weights and measurements and sizes handed out to fatties who want to look like anorexics.

"How are you doing?" asks the clerk.

"Terrible," Ellen says. "This suit won't button. It looks terrible. Do you have it in an 18?"

"We don't carry 18s," she answers.

There is silence while Ellen actually contemplates that she is willing to buy a size 18. It is an epiphany, a moment of revelation that she has gone from a size 5 at 18 years old to a size 18 at 41 years old. Like the salesclerk, Ellen used to be a size 5. The clerk looks about 35 years old; she wears wool Bermuda shorts and knee socks.

"We do have several dresses that would be very nice. You haven't looked at our dresses. Would you like me to bring you an Anne Pinkerton? The line runs big and it's quite smart."

"Yes," Ellen says. "That would be fine. Bring me a dress." To the mirror she says, bring me a tent.

The salesclerk hands the dress to Ellen, opening the dressing room door only slightly. "The blue wool will look nice with your coloring, I think. It will be lovely with your hair."

Ellen mutters.

"Pardon?"

"Nothing," Ellen says. She thinks again about the window. She thinks about what's behind the window. She hums a line from her favorite song. She thinks about Jack. How she would have hummed that line to him. But he wouldn't have liked it. He didn't like anything she liked. She is kind of glad he is dead. That way, she didn't have to leave him. He left her first. But she resents the finality. The way he did it.

Lines of songs race through her head. When Ellen was young, her mother used to sing one line of a song after Ellen's father left: "He didn't even ... say he was leaving." Her mother would laugh when she sang that line and Ellen never understood why. Oh, how the memories return. The white wooden table in the kitchen where the radio sat, playing country music. The kick her mom would get out of the silliest lines. Lines of songs that meant nothing to Ellen. But now she knows. Because now lines from tunes stick in Ellen's head and surface without her knowing it.

She hums them, laughs at them, and her daughter says, "I don't think that's funny. Why do you laugh when you sing that?" Right now, her daughter disapproves of her singing lines from the Talking Heads. "I've changed my hair style so many times, I don't know what I look like."

Ellen takes off the suit skirt, struggles to remove it over her stomach, which hangs like a pale pillow of puffed rice. Seersucker stomach, Jack said once. The most creative line he ever uttered, Ellen thinks.

"How are you doing?" asks the clerk.

"Fine, fine," Ellen answers. She doesn't want the clerk to find her inside the dressing room, taupe suit in a heap, ugly large blue wool dress not even off the hanger.

Though she doesn't want to look, in her boredom, she peeks behind the Laura Ashley curtains. Across the street is the drugstore.

"I used to live in that apartment across the street," Ellen says. The door is closed, and she does not know if the clerk hears her. There is no answer. Ellen continues. "It was a horrible time in my life. But I was thin. I really don't think I appreciated it though. Not my weight. And certainly not my husband. But he's dead now." There is silence for a while. Ellen looks out the window, regresses to the time when she and Jack lived there. How awful. It was little and dark. And all those steps. She remembers lugging groceries and laundry up them. Outside staircase. Above the drugstore. Aqua-swirled carpet. She hated it. Small rooms. No window in the bedroom. But there was a window in the living room. Plants. She had a rubber tree plant and it grew and grew. What happened to it, she wonders.

"How's the dress?"

"Oh, I'm not quite ready yet." Ellen slips the dress off the hanger, covers her body, which looks lumpy and pasty like the Pillsbury Dough Boy. She wears the blue wool and stares out the window. The building oozes with memories. Jack drinking. Jack wanting to have babies. Lots of them. Jack never staying home. Clipped words. No conversations.

Jack, when he worked, was an engineer. Engineers didn't talk. They didn't talk and they couldn't write, according to Jack. They drew specifications and made everyone else live by them. Save money for a rainy day. Save money for a house. Waste no money on the arts. Ellen felt like she had almost died. When she would finally talk Jack into seeing a movie, the thrill was gone. He didn't enjoy it and she had to baby him, cajole him, trick him, to get to go to a film. No room for play. No room for the frivolous. Shopping used to be a nightmare. She used to change the price tags when she bought things. She lied. She would have had to change these price tags for sure.

"How are you doing? Would you like to show me the dress?"

The door opens, even though Ellen hasn't answered the clerk's question.

"That looks nice. Here, let me help you with that bow." The clerk ties it.

"Very nice. And very businesslike, too. Don't you think?"

"It is a nice dress. I like the material. But I don't know. I don't like this color on me." The color reminds her of something. Jack's wedding suit?

"It's lovely. Very flattering, don't you think?"

"Well ..." Ellen turns in the mirror a bit. "Let me think for a while about it."

The clerk leaves.

Ellen looks out the window again, tries to reconstruct her life in the dress shop. That's what she would have done with the insurance money if Jack had had any — open a dress shop. But he was unemployed at the time he got shot. The gun backfired. Shot in some field near Havana. He was duck hunting. She remembers his ugly green and brown hunting outfits. His duck call. He used to leave early in the morning, come home late at night — drunk. One night, he never came home at all. Sometimes she misses him.

For a long time, she watched for him at 5 o'clock when he would come home from work or from the tavern down the street. But this time, he never came back. Except in her dreams. Then he talked. He told her what death was like. For a while, she thought of joining him, but she couldn't leave her daughter. She wonders if, in heaven, they serve drinks, watch football.

"Have you decided on the dress?"

"No, I'm still thinking." Ellen hears the footsteps of the clerk as she walks away. She knows that the clerk knows that she is not concentrating on buying new clothes. But why should she? The suits don't fit and the dress looks like something Jack's mother would have worn. Not that there was anything wrong with Jack's mother. But she wasn't the fashion queen of the year.

Once, Ellen had been the fashion queen of the year at college. She had been elected the most fashionable girl on campus her freshman year at college. It was a small college; most of the students were from the Midwest — farm towns. They didn't exactly rival the best-dressed at Sarah Lawrence. That's where Ellen had wanted to go to school.

She used to pore through the magazines — *Seventeen, Mademoiselle, Vogue, Glamour* — pretend she was someone else. Pretend she was a fashion writer. Pretend she was Gloria Steinem. Gloria was on the cover of *Glamour* in the '60s; Ellen thought Gloria Steinem was the prettiest woman she had ever seen. Although at the time, Ellen would have said "girl." There was something about her smile, something romantic. Ellen idolized her, wrote her adoring letters, asked her what it was like to be her. But Ellen never sent the letters because she thought she was so insignificant that Gloria would say, "Who are you? How dare you write to me?" She kept her fan letters to herself, created a pile labeled "Letters to Gloria."

Years later, when Ellen raised her consciousness (the early '70s), she and Gloria connected again. But it would still have sounded funny to send the letters. "Dear Gloria," she would begin. "You don't know me, but our paths have, in a way, developed along the same lines. Except you are prettier, thinner, and you have more power, prestige and money. Other than that, we are sisters. I've loved you from afar."

She still wrote letters, padded the ever-thick pile, loved Gloria from afar. Every time someone said something about Gloria, it was like a personal insult to Ellen. Ellen would defend her. She's just perfect, Ellen would say.

"How is the dress? Have you decided? Can I bring you anything else?"

"Um, not yet." Ellen looks at the price tag. She might buy it just to save herself some embarrassment. It is an expensive price tag. The tag hangs from lavender silk thread; it is pinned on the garment with a tiny gold safety pin. It will be expensive. Ellen has spent enough time in dressing rooms to know that when the tags are that good, things are expensive. Besides, the dress feels good. The color is bad, but the material has something besides wool in it. It is soft and clingy. It clings to the lumps on her thighs, to her large breasts. She almost likes that. Maybe she should show off what she does have. She at least likes her breasts. The tag says, "We hand-embroidered and crocheted the trim on this bodice in New England. Dry clean only. $376."

"No, I don't think so." Ellen slips the dress over her head, hands it out the door to the clerk. "The color is not quite right, and to be honest, the price isn't either. This dress is $376."

"Yes. But you get what you pay for, you know. And if you are looking for a dress to wear to work, this really is perfect."

"I like it. I really do. But I was looking for a light wool suit. And I just can't spend this much on a dress. Really."

Ellen stands for a moment, facing the clerk, holding her blouse over her fat white globby stomach, which reminds her of mounds of flesh-colored jello.

"Is there anything else I can show you?"

"No, I don't think so. I'm going to get dressed and look around."

"That's a good idea. We have an entire room that you haven't seen yet."

Ellen half-heartedly gets dressed, looks out the window the entire time. The drugstore brings back memories. She remembers the thick chocolate milk shakes the old man who owned the store used to make. He used to tease her and tease her — until Jack's drinking problem became obvious to him too, and then he teased her less and less.

Ellen pulls on her pants, slacks with an elastic waistline — a new feature of her playclothes since she has gained 40 pounds. She doesn't have much desire to lose the 40 pounds. It doesn't seem to interfere with her life much, except that she can't buy clothes, but then she doesn't have a lot of money to spend anyway. The fat keeps men away, Ellen notices. And she doesn't want a man. It wasn't just Jack. It was even after Jack. After his death, Ellen became thin. A lot of men were interested in her. Men piled up like cigarettes — some consumed, some discarded halfway, some burned out completely.

She went through a period which she casually referred to as her sport-fucking stage. Now, it shocks her to think about it. AIDS is integrating itself into society like busing. First, it is Haitians, hemophiliacs and homosexuals, but soon it will be everybody.

She leaves the dressing room.

Ellen will not expose herself to the plague. Better to be fat and celibate. Rolls of fat ripple as she buttons her blouse.

In the shop are women who look like they belong. They have blonde hair — short, fashionable haircuts, blunt cuts. They wear navy and burgundy wool, argyle sweater vests. All of them are thin. They stand on the Oriental carpets, lounge on the wicker chaise, pick among the scarves in the glass case.

Ellen stops at the socks. There are all kinds of socks in a basket on the counter. She can afford socks and her feet are not much bigger. Though they do hurt most of the time from carrying her weight — a new problem, Ellen thinks, brought on by 40 extra pounds.

"These are lovely socks," Ellen says to no one in particular.

The clerk is within proximity, but she does not respond. She probably does not get a commission on socks, Ellen thinks.

She examines each pair. There is a pair of Christmas tree socks. Red with green trim and green pine trees. Once, she bought her two sisters a pair like these. It may have been the only present she ever brought them that they liked.

There is a pair with an elk or a moose — gray and white with brown trim on the antlers. The socks remind her of Jack. Jack liked gray and brown. With the exception of one red and green plaid flannel shirt, all his clothes had been gray, brown, olive green. Three colors, all dark and muted. Once she had bought him a pink shirt, a red-checked shirt and white corduroy pants. He took them all back and got a gray, black and brown plaid wool jacket. It was dark and ugly and itchy. Ellen hated it. He loved it.

What happened to that jacket? She remembers burying her head in it once at the movies when a scary part came on screen. *Whatever Happened to Baby Jane* was the movie. Ellen's long hair, brown then, got caught in the zipper.

The salesclerk stares at Ellen, who holds the socks and is back at the movie in 1962.

"Yes? Would you like to buy those socks?"

"Uh, no ... well ... I ... might, but I'm just looking." She picks up another pair — aqua, red and yellow trimmed in beige leather. "I'll take these socks," she says, and proudly hands them over to the clerk. She wants more socks. She fantasizes about spending $248 on socks. That's how much she would have paid for a suit. She wonders how many pairs of socks she could buy for $248. The whole basket?

A basket of socks. Which she can't even wear to work. What a waste. Jack would have frowned on spending $248 on socks. A lot of socks. Now she is thinking about the words *a lot*. It is a phrase people use in memos at the office: "There is a lot of talk going around about the new conversion." "A lot is a plot of ground" is what her English teacher said in grammar school.

And there is Jack, only five miles away from the dress shop, from the old apartment, in the cold brown-black Illinois soil on the prairie where he was born and raised. And where, if he hadn't liked to hunt squirrel, rabbits, deer and duck, he might still be, above the drugstore. Although surely he would have built a house by now. He would have planted white pines, his favorite tree. On a lot. A lot is a plot of ground.

Ellen threw a rose in his open grave, whispered good-bye, let the cold wind roll around her, held onto the baby, called good-bye while her family softly murmured among themselves that she was not right. Her intellectual sister, who was pretentious and loved to use big words to confuse others, said that Ellen had dementia praecox. Ellen figured she got that out of a night school class at Northwestern U in Chicago, or she had recently watched a Tennessee Williams film.

Ellen didn't have dementia praecox. What she had was a lot of anger. A lot is a plot of ground. She had a lot of anger. Which didn't leave for a long time. And which, when she looks at those socks, is brought home again. She puts them back.

"It's a difficult day for decisions, huh?"

"Yes," Ellen says to the clerk. "Yes, it is. These socks are nice, but they remind me of my late husband."

"I'm sorry," says the clerk.

"Don't be," Ellen says. "I'm not. It's better this way."

The clerk gives her a funny look, a look Ellen has seen before. A look that says, don't say inappropriate things in the dress shop. You're supposed to purchase items of apparel in here. Not lose reality.

Maybe she should leave this town, paint this town black in her mind, frame it in gilded memories.

But she has tried that. In the early days, after Jack's death, she thought she fell in love with a hippie. But he wasn't a hippie; he was a drug addict. She was stuck in San Jose, living in a rented house in the suburbs where the neighbors didn't speak to her because they didn't like transients and where he played his music so loud that they thought she was poor white trash. That's how they behaved. She was depressed, so she read magazines all day and looked at how she thought life should have been and wasn't. She wanted to be the woman in the ad, the one who wore the right perfume, who didn't have body odor or pores let alone moles or chipped nail polish on her toes. Ellen wanted to stand, in a white slinky evening dress, next to a Peugeot and drink Chivas Regal.

Instead, she sat in a brown plastic beanbag chair, which reminded her of a pile of shit. (It was purchased at the Thrift-i-Mart). On a good day, she ate macaroni and cheese. On a bad day, peanut butter on crackers. Her daughter went to school every day, so she didn't have to face what was happening at home. What was happening was that Ellen realized that she had made a terrible mistake. She had lost Jack and found J.D., and he was worse than Jack.

He lay on the couch day after day, caught up in his own "wows" and smoking marijuana. When he couldn't afford good dope, he went out on the streets and snorted and pushed angel dust. He was away a lot. When he was home, he was on the couch watching some marvelous revelation on TV. Wow.

After six months of wows, women and wonderful experiences (for him), Ellen and her daughter left. Came home. To the prairie, where the soil actually smelled like rich dirt, where the streets were narrow and the sky was plentiful. Where the cicadas sang and where there were no fleas and where Ellen could grow broccoli. Ellen stayed with her friend Star, who was earthy and natural. She taught Ellen how to take care of plants and kids, how to be mellow without drugs and how to be nice. Star would like the socks with the bright colors. But she is in China now, studying herbal medicine. In quest of the ginseng.

"The socks are $15.78," says the clerk. "Cash or charge?"

"American Express. But don't ring it up yet. I have to look at the earrings."

"They are in the next room," the clerk says.

Ellen leaves the counter, leaves the basket of socks. She hears someone say something. She hopes they don't talk about her. She wishes they understood what it's like to try on a thousand suits and have them all be too small.

The earrings are in a basket on a table. There is a sale. Ellen finds a pair — cut glass balls, like globes. Shiny and sparkly. She has to have them. Only $2.50. Nothing else in the place is for sale for that amount. She loves them. She puts them back in the basket. They are not practical. Where can she wear them? Not to work. The publications editor in a frumpy size-18 dress with glass globes? But only $2.50.

Ellen reminds herself of the purpose of the trip. This shopping trip is supposed to net a wool business suit. If you buy earrings, she tells herself, buy gold ones — gold hoops like the girls in the shop are wearing. They are the rich, the crème de la crème, of this prairie town. They know how to dress. You can never go wrong with gold earrings, Ellen reminds herself. They are tasteful. Glass balls, she tells herself. Really. She puts them down, picks up a pair of gold earrings. They are too heavy; they will weigh on her dainty lobes — the only place that hasn't gotten fatter through the years.

Ah, but here are some. Large. Like a painter's palette. Red, splashes of green, touches of blue. They are the big kind, the flat kind, the kind that plaster to her ears, that attract attention, that detract from her weight.

Ten dollars. Not too bad, she thinks. Twenty-five dollars for socks and earrings. And she doesn't need either. She needs a suit.

"Will that be all?" says the clerk in a voice that implies she hopes so.

"Yes. That's all."

"Sign here, please."

"Thank you for bringing me all those clothes. You have been very helpful."

"That's my job," says the clerk. "Do come back if you want the blue dress."

"I want the taupe suit. I think I'll go to Weight Watchers. I'm tired of buying socks and earrings. I'll give up smoking and reading novels. I'll eat yogurt and run in the park."

"Smoking and reading novels. Oh dear." The clerk moves back. She recovers. "Our new line is coming in next week. We will have a trunk showing on Tuesday at 3. It's a line that runs rather large. You may find something. Do come."

"That sounds great," Ellen says. "I'll try to come in."

She knows she will not come for the showing. The last time she came, they served white wine and Brie cheese. Ellen ate all the cheese, drank most of the wine, went back to work a little woozy. The skinny blonde rich women drank black coffee. Ellen will not be back for the trunk showing. They never show socks and earrings.

Don't Get Me Wrong

Ellen sits in the laundromat waiting for her clothes to finish washing when she hears the song.

"Oh don't get me wrong ... it's just that I am not in the market for a girl who wants to love only me ... and I ain't saying you ain't pretty ..."

The song brings back memories. Ellen remembers that song and in turn remembers her life 10 years ago. A blue-eyed musician. Danny. She remembers flirting, flirting. She remembers nights in a steamy car in the Fast Track Lounge parking lot, groping, moaning, steaming up the window with hot breathy puffs of passion. She remembers she was married. She remembers so was he.

Ellen watches the people in the laundromat, finds their behavior curious. A man makes furtive calls from a pay phone. He writes phone numbers on the wall, waits for a return call. He talks loudly, asks if Linda is there. When will she be there? His syntax needs work. He does not pronounce his *g*'s, says *anyways*, says *don't* for *doesn't*. Ellen fights off the urge to correct his grammar, to set things right.

The washing machine shimmies and shakes. Soap suds seep out the bottom and line the machine. A bubble carpet. Did she put the soap in twice? Ellen does not remember.

She does remember when she first noticed Danny, who was singing at the Fast Track. What were the words she used to describe the game? Putting the make on? Scoring? It was like a game. The stakes were high. Ellen didn't know how high.

"Oh don't get me wrong ... it's just that I am not in the market for a boy who wants to love only me. And I ain't saying you ain't pretty. All I'm saying is I'm not ready ..."

Ellen wasn't ready. Wasn't ready for an affair, wasn't ready for sex, wasn't ready for a divorce, but it happened anyway. Danny left his wife, Ellen left her husband, and for what? Two good years together and all of a sudden she pulled in the reins and he began singing other places, nights in bars on roads in hotel rooms with other women who played his instruments as well as he did and like she couldn't. They argued publicly everywhere — in the Fast Track, in the supermarket, in the laundromat.

The washer stops. Ellen transfers the wet laundry into the cart. She has four loads — one whites, one darks, one towels, one rags.

One of the rags is the muslin dress she used to wear with Danny. It was his favorite. Ivory with an appliquéd brown bird. She remembers wearing that dress with brown Bass sandals. She loved sandals. Even more, she loved going barefoot. Danny frowned on going barefoot. He talked of dangers and germs, of disease. Ellen liked the feel of things underfoot.

Ellen puts quarters in the dryer. She remembers 10 years ago she used dimes. She remembers the snow falling steadily on a night like tonight.

What was the holiday they spent together? New Year's Eve? Ellen remembers being snowed in — she was still married at that time. Where was her husband Jack? In Canada, ice fishing?

"And I'm not saying you ain't pretty. All I'm saying is I'm not ready..."

Ellen wasn't sure whether she wanted to stay married to Jack and have torrid affairs with stray musicians. Or if she wanted to drop Jack and marry Danny. Or if she wanted to look around. Although if she had listened to the voices inside her, she would have realized that she did want to leave Jack and she didn't need Danny to leave Jack. But she wasn't there yet, wasn't even close. To her, a man was a man was a man and a woman had to have one. She had to have one. Jack or Danny?

At least with Danny, she could sit in bars instead of on the ice. And it was entertaining to watch the night show, to watch the pickups, to see the groupies, to see the girls make over Danny, to see him prefer her. She was exactly what he wanted. She had everything he wanted. At least for a while.

Ellen resents the man next to her who is smoking. His smoke smells cheap and cancerous. She wants to tell him to stop. After all, she has stopped smoking. His smoking reminds her of how much she loves strong, non-filtered cigarettes — Camels, English Ovals. She waves the smoke away, hoping he'll pay attention to her non-verbals, but he does not notice or care. To curb her rising anger, Ellen tries to become interested in something else besides a stranger's smoke. She picks up a copy of *Newsweek*. She flips through it, reads "My Turn" and scans current affairs.

She checks the clothes, watches torn underwear toss around in the dryer. She remembers riding in the dryers when she was younger, remembers mostly the fear. She remembers when she cared about her underwear, remembers the underwear Danny bought her.

Ellen stands by the dryer. A little boy looks for money under the washers. Amidst the lint, he finds dimes and quarters.

Danny was blonde and blue-eyed and so young and cute. Ellen wonders why he was interested in her, but looking back 10 years ago, she was pretty cute herself. He was a little shorter than she was. That, she thinks, is her lot in life. To be attracted to short men. She is 5 feet 9 inches tall. Recently, Ellen saw a talk show about short men and all the women called in to say nasty things to short men. Ellen wanted to call in and tell the talk show host that she liked short men, preferred short men. But she did not call.

"Oh don't get me wrong ... it's just that I am not in the market for a girl who wants to love only me ..."

What was the title of that song? "Different Drum?" Danny was the first musician in a long line of lovers who came later. He was the lead singer — vocals. He was the first and only singer. Much later, Ellen got involved with a bassist, a drummer, a sax player. There was a pronounced difference between vocals and instruments. Eventually, Danny didn't talk. Like everyone who makes a living with words, he began to hoard them.

His voice, when he sang though, was soft and rhythmic.

"Oh don't get me wrong ... I'm not ready for any person, place or thing to try and pull the reins in on me ..."

He sang, sweetly, until Ellen put him in a cage and he stopped. He was unhappy; he couldn't sing. Looking back, Ellen didn't blame him. She hadn't been happy either.

She skims the current issue of *Newsweek*. The dryers stop. She puts down the magazine. She is tired of reading about the trouble in the Gulf, about failures.

Triple-Word Sting

Ellen watches Ernesto take his turn at Scrabble. The board balances delicately on the white wicker bed tray that sits between them. He thinks, index finger to his mouth. He wears a gray T-shirt that is too small and pulls around the middle; it says "Harvard."

Ellen turns the timer upside down and watches the sands shift through the hourglass.

"Your turn is almost up," she says, rousing Ernesto from his reverie. He takes his time placing his letters on the board. He spells *than* — worth 12 points.

Ellen has a word ready. She thinks more quickly than Ernesto, and every once in a while she feels superior because of her speed. She spells *viola* for 12 points.

Ernesto studies the Scrabble board. The timer runs.

"I don't know how you can leave me with so little opportunity here," he says.

Ellen cannot believe she is hearing right. They have been playing Scrabble for 10 years and he has never given her any opportunities. He adds *s*'s and *d*'s to the words she makes. It irritates Ellen and it has for 10 years. Ernesto pauses.

"I know," he says. "I'm too stupid to figure out a word."

Ellen fights the desire to tell him he is right. She has never heard him admit to any weakness, let alone stupidity — which, in Ellen's opinion, is not his problem at all. Still, she fights off the desire to agree. She wants to tell him that he is not stupid, just slow. Telling Ernesto he is slow would not accomplish anything.

When she met him 10 years ago in a biology class, he was a half hour late every morning. She couldn't understand it. He would walk in slowly, calling attention to himself. It was hard not to notice Ernesto. His hair was long, black, silky and tied in a ponytail at the time. He wore panchos and vests that looked like Mexican blankets. Colorful. He was a leftover hippie and, to be truthful, at that time Ellen didn't look much better herself. But she came to class on time so no one would notice.

Once, Ellen and Ernesto went on vacation together to Tampa. They went to visit her sister Duffy Jo. The night before they left, Ernesto got drunk and arrived home at 5 a.m. The plane left St. Louis, an hour and a half away, at 6:30 a.m. Somehow, they made it on time. Ernesto was frightened of the airplane — a fact he had forgotten to tell Ellen. He turned green and puked all the way to Tampa.

"I only have two vowels," Ernesto moans.

"Don't make excuses," Ellen says. "Play. Your turn is almost up."

She is hard. Maybe it's her job. As a management consultant, she has gotten so used to telling people what to do and looking for results that she forgets she is not in a business deal.

He spells *kit* for 17.

"Please pass the letters," Ernesto says. His voice is controlled. The box of letters is controlled too, by either Ernesto or Ellen — both of whom place the box underneath their respective sides of the wicker couch. When it's Ellen's turn, she puts the box under her side; when it's Ernesto's, he puts it under his side. Ellen hates having to ask for anything, especially Scrabble letters that belong to her.

Ellen has the *q*. She wants to spell a word with it, but she does not have a *u*. She cannot think of one.

"Your turn is up," Ernesto says, pointing to the hourglass. There are no grains of sand left. The sand sits heaving, like the *q* in Ellen's Scrabble tray.

"That's not fair," Ellen protests.

"It's the rule," Ernesto says, fingering his mustache. "That's what we decided to go by."

Ellen sulks. She pulls at her hair, examining the long multicolored strands as if she expected to find something in them. While she pulls a strand of hair apart, she studies the board looking for an open *u*. Ernesto spells *eyed* for 14. Ellen spots a *q*, but it isn't in a profitable place. She wants to get the most she can and this spot doesn't have a double-word or double-letter score, let alone a triple-word score. She puts a *t, r, d* next to the *u*.

"Turd," Ernesto mocks. "What kind of word is that?"

"I don't care," Ellen says defiantly. "It's not pretty, but it's all I could do. Give me the letters."

Ernesto pulls the box out from under his side of the couch. Ellen grabs it aggressively.

"You don't have to get shitty about it because you spelled *turd.*" Ernesto smirks at his own pun. This is what he lives for, Ellen thinks — to laugh at his own puns. Ellen wants to tell him he's too gamy. She scowls at him instead.

"You are the champion of smut Scrabble," he says.

She watches the timer, thinking that if life is fair, his time will run out and he'll have to miss his turn like she did. He spells *volts* for 12. Ellen sees an opening — not for her *q*, but for *ponds* and *skits*, worth 28 points.

Ernesto fingers his lips. Ellen splits hairs. The timer runs. As the last grain of sand runs through the glass, Ernesto spells *damn* for 13 points.

"It's not okay for me to spell *turd*, but it's okay for you to spell *damn*, huh? You have situational ethics," Ellen says. She spies an open *u*. She quickly spells *quip* for 28 points. She is happy to get rid of the *q*. Holding it is like getting stuck with the Old Maid.

"I have situational letters, not situational ethics," Ernesto explains, leaning forward to add an *e* to the beginning of Ellen's word *quip*.

"What's the score?" he asks, leaning back on the couch.

"You have 103; I have 98," Ellen says. He looks pleased.

Ellen studies the board. She eyes an open space on a triple-word score. She places her letters in the squares and spells *jeep*, using Ernesto's *e* from *equip* — 64 points.

She has 162; he has 103. He spells *bing* for 14. They are not speaking. The phone rings. Ellen stands up to run to the phone. She is barefoot and something stings her left foot; it feels like she stepped on a lit cigarette. She runs to the phone anyway; she cannot let a phone ring.

It is her sister Duffy Jo, calling long distance. Duffy wants to know two things: one, why she has not received a dishtowel from the dishtowel chain letter; two, how Ellen likes the bridge in her mouth.

"I don't know why you didn't get a dishtowel," Ellen says. "Who wants to send a dishtowel in the mail? I don't know anyone who cares about doing such a thing. If Aunt Sarah hadn't sent the letter, I never would have responded to it. But since Uncle Morris died, I figure if she wants a dishtowel, I'll send her one and send out the letter. Although I had trouble finding five friends to send it to. And I don't think any of the five followed up on it."

"Yeah," Duffy admits. "I had trouble finding people to send it to, too. Maybe they didn't follow up on it. But I did. I bought an expensive dishtowel and sent it to the first name on the list."

Ellen makes a mental note to send Duffy Jo a dishtowel. Duffy has always complained that Ellen got more than she did as a child. It may have been true, but the family was so dysfunctional that no one got too much. Once Ellen read a workbook about shame-based families and her family had every characteristic that was listed in the book.

"Do you mind if I ask you a personal question?" Duffy says. This strikes Ellen as odd, since Duffy knows everything about Ellen's life.

"It's a subject you are sensitive to," Duffy says.

"Money?" Ellen questions.

"No. Teeth. How do you like your bridge?"

"Fine, great. I love my bridge over troubled tongue," Ellen jokes. "But that's not very personal. Why do you ask?"

Duffy asks so she can elaborate about the extensive dental work that she is considering. Ellen listens.

At the end of the conversation, Ellen tells Duffy, "I think maybe I stepped on a bee. My foot hurts."

"Make a paste of baking soda and water and put it on the sting," Duffy says. Ellen assures Duffy she will do this, although she does not intend to follow through. She cannot leave the Scrabble game long enough to make a paste.

Ernesto is still thinking about a word when Ellen arrives on the porch.

"I've been gone so long," she says. "Haven't you spelled a word yet?" She wonders how anyone can be so slow. The only time Ernesto's pace benefits Ellen, she thinks, is when they make love. Right now she doesn't even feel like thinking about it. She is angry at him as he ponders his next turn. Ellen turns the timer right side up again.

"When that sand is gone, so is your turn," she says maliciously. "You are not getting any free rides. What's good for the goose is good for the gander." She is still mad about missing her turn when he is the slow one. Plus, he doesn't open up the board. He adds endings to her words: *s, d, ing.*

"Thank you for your compassion," Ernesto says sarcastically. He moves his block of letters around on his tray. He counts the number of open squares on the triple-letter score. As the last grain of sand leaves the glass, Ernesto spells *no* and *oiled* in a triple-word score for 23. "What's the score?" he asks.

"You, 166. Me, 202."

She has spelled *fine, heart, hers, rage, girl.* He has spelled *feet, swan, axe, rye, ba.* She tries to understand why this game makes them fight. Before they began to play Scrabble, they were talking about living together. Now she cannot even imagine such a situation. He is slow. He won't open up the board. He tries to spell words that are not words. She challenges him and usually she is right. She stakes out a special spot for her letters and he puts his letters in it. It will never work, she knows. Maybe that's what she hates about this game. It makes her look at all the things she ignores.

"Maybe we shouldn't play Scrabble anymore," Ernesto says, as if he is reading her mind. "We always fight. Maybe we should get rid of this game."

Ellen is not ready to do that. "No," she says. "We just need to realize it's a game. That's all."

Flag Day

It was so hot, Ellen spent her evenings figuring out ways to get out of her third-floor apartment. It was so hot, Ellen could not even stand to wear underwear. Panty hose. A bracelet. Anything on her body was too hot. Ellen took off all her clothes, paraded around naked, laughed at her fat bouncing.

Across the hallway, Ellen could hear her neighbor Ernesto singing. She could hear him because the building was built in a horseshoe; their bedroom and bathroom windows faced one another. Ellen kept her windows shuttered and closed up; Ernesto didn't care. He didn't have shutters, drapes or curtains. He had an active sex life.

Once, Ellen had slept with him. Ernie carried a knife, a switchblade, which Ellen found exciting. A blade under the pillow. Ellen liked risks, liked danger. She didn't like the heat, didn't like the suffocation.

Ellen wrapped herself in a long beach towel — black with a pink flamingo on it. She had safely secured the towel around her when she decided to go over to Ernie. He would be surprised. Ellen had not sought him out in months. He had too many women. Ellen could not have a relationship with him. He said his women friends were just friends. But Ellen could hear them at night. "You have too many friends for things to be peaceful," Ellen told Ernesto. He didn't agree. Life was peaceful for him, he said.

But Ernesto had air conditioning and Ellen did not. Ellen knocked on his door. Ernie didn't hear. He was singing; she could hear him. His voice boomed. Ernie the performer. What a shame he was not able to perform during the day, in his real-life job. In real life, he worked at the post office. In his secret life, he sang, acted, carried knives, made love to loads of women.

"Ernie," Ellen called. "Ernie."

She knocked hard on the glass panes and kicked the oak door frame. It seemed like she stood there for several minutes. Finally,

Ernesto walked by and noticed her in the hall, knocking. He opened the door. Ellen stepped in. A blast of cool air welcomed her.

"What brings you here, my chiquita?" Ernie asked. He had a burgundy towel wrapped around the lower half of his body.

"Oh, nothing much," Ellen said. She stood, looked around, searched for signs of women — an earring, a shoe, a roach, a cigarette butt with lipstick.

Ernie stared at her. "We're both wearing towels," he said. "What does that mean?" He stayed his ground, didn't advance. Ellen was glad; she wanted to hold him at bay.

"It means I'm hot," Ellen said. "Which is why I came over. I am too hot to wear clothes. Especially underwear."

"I'm glad you didn't," Ernie said, looking her up and down. "I've never seen you in a towel. The colors are very becoming."

Ellen held the towel tightly to her. She fingered objects. A candle, pink, shaped like a large breast. A teacup with primroses. A statue of a fertility god.

"Sit down, sit down. Get comfortable. Would you like a beer?" Ernie pushed his black silk hair from his face. Ellen fixated on the pores of his skin — big, deep, like holes. He was tan, so tan. Looking at him made her remember his kiss, his touch, his large pulsating cock.

"Would you like a beer?" He asked the question again, his voice lowered. His eyes seemed to peer into her mind. She was sure he could see what she was thinking, sure he could see it vividly, like a show, a technicolor video.

"A beer? No, I don't think so. Do you have any iced tea?" Ellen brought herself back, tried to think sensibly.

"I don't have iced tea. I have papaya juice. Would you like some?"

"No thanks. I'll have a beer." She paused. "Please." Ellen smiled at Ernie. He looked at her ... with longing?

Papaya. Ernie was the only man she knew who kept a steady supply of beer, papaya and sinsemilla. That was about all.

Papaya reminded her of Mexico, reminded her of the time she almost died from eating fresh papaya, reminded her of sickness, fever, the runs, the Aztec two-step. She thought, at the time, she would die. Mexico. Where she met a man like Ernie who was not Ernie, but was like Ernie. Mario. She remembered the good and the bad, the highs and the lows. Making love, making love, making love. Getting sick, getting sick, getting sick.

Ernesto handed Ellen a beer. Dos XX. Her least favorite kind. It was strong and hot and dark.

"Would you like anything else?" he asked politely. There was something seductive about his tone, about the question.

Ellen looked him up and down. "Not right now," she said. Her eyes focused on a bulge under his maroon towel, his dark silk hair. He pushed it out of his eyes, held his beer in the air.

"To the heat," he said.

"To Flag Day," Ellen said. She forced the strong liquid down her hot, constricted throat.

"Would you like to smoke?" he asked.

She didn't want to. "No thanks. I don't smoke anymore."

"Good. That's good. Cigarettes are bad for you. But this ..." He pulled a joint out of a cigar box, which was hiding behind a large unabridged dictionary. "... is good for you."

Ernie sat down on the sofa next to her.

Ellen looked around the apartment. There wasn't much to look at. He had records, records, records and an old gray saggy sofa. In the bedroom, she knew, was an old mattress on the floor. It was indeed the '80s, but Ernie wasn't changing his old '60s habits. There was no decor, to speak of, in this place. Everything looked like a garage sale item, a piece too old to use, a Sal Arms bargain.

Ernie smoked. He held the joint out to Ellen like an offering.

Ellen took it. "I don't think I need this. The beer is strong enough."

"For what?"

"What?"

"For what? Strong enough for what? To help you relax?"

"Yes. To help me relax." The words came out, but Ellen was totally confused about what they meant. What was happening to her? His damn dope. What was in it? Was it the heat? The beer? The smoke? His smell?

He lit a stick of incense, sat back on the sofa. His legs, spread apart, revealed purplish black testicles. Ellen began to laugh. She thought of a joke about testicles, a joke one of her best friends always told. Her friend, who was so proper, telling this joke. It was so funny to Ellen. She laughed some more.

Ernie laughed too and passed her the joint again. He leaned over to pass it. She could smell him. She hoped he couldn't smell her. She stank. Smelled like hair and sweat.

Ellen continued to laugh. "My friend's favorite joke," Ellen said. "You know what one testicle said to the other? What are we doing hanging here when the guy in the middle did the shooting?" Out loud, it sounded even funnier. Ellen laughed again.

Ernie laughed. They laughed together.

"What's the answer?" he said. He leaned over again, placed the joint between Ellen's lips.

"To what?"

"The riddle."

"It's not a riddle."

"It's not?"

"No. It's a joke."

"Is that all?"

"Yes. That's all."

"The guy in the middle wants to do a little shooting. Can you tell?"

Ellen gulped. Nodded. Stared at Ernie's swollen member reaching up under the towel.

Ernesto moved closer. Undid her towel. Began to feel her breasts, lick her nipples. "Your breasts are large cantaloupes," he said. Ellen closed her eyes. She relaxed on the saggy sofa. Ernie coaxed her inverted nipple out; it became a round hard ball. He licked and licked. She lost consciousness, briefly. His fingers were inside her. He was humming. She was focusing on his fingers. "Your cunt opens up like a ballroom," he whispered.

"Dance me inside," she said.

"Dance me inside," he said. He played with her labia, fingered her magic button. "Dance me inside," he said again. He hummed bars from "Dance with Me" by the Drifters.

Ellen wanted to explain that she could not take credit for those words. She wanted to tell Ernie that she stole the words from William Kinsella from his book of stories, *Dance Me Outside*. But Ellen was beyond explanations. She was reduced to a juicy pulp, an overripe plum, bruised, decaying, juice oozing from her skin.

"Dance me inside," Ernie repeated as he climbed on top of her. He pointed his pulsing purple member into her moist orifice. He moved. And moved. Slowly.

Ellen could smell herself on his fingers. Sour.

"I smell," she whispered while he danced. "Sour."

"Sweet and sour," he said, moving, moving, humming bars of "Swing Low, Sweet Chariot."

They became two bodies moving like one, dancing, dancing, dancing, calling, humming, moaning, dancing. Then silent. She came. He came. They came.

In the morning, Ellen went home, across the hall. She turned on the fan, took a bath, washed his hot sperm from her burning cunt. She could hardly walk. It was only June. Flag Day. What would she do if the heat continued?

The Fourth of July

It was another memory Ellen didn't want, another memory she could have done without. But each time she set out to do a task, here it was — another memory, like a slug, crawling into her consciousness. The scene was a kitchen. It was Saturday, July 4, and Ellen had just picked blueberries. She had nine pounds of blueberries and nothing to do with them. She made a pot of coffee, rummaged through her bottom kitchen drawer looking for recipes, looking for blueberry buckle. Ellen had, over the years, collected an odd assortment, and an even odder arrangement, of recipes. While she promised herself, each time she looked for something, that she would buy a small recipe book and type these recipes up on cards, she found that she did not do that. She had never done it. The recipes lay in five large manila folders, separated into four categories: meat dishes, casseroles, dessert and miscellaneous. Ellen was looking for blueberry buckle.

Instead she found a white, lined piece of paper with a note on it that said: "Dear Ernesto, I know you wonder each day we wake up together whether I will be the Beauty or the Beast." The note ended there. It was on the same paper as a recipe for Mexican marinated fish: 2 pounds red snapper, 1/2 cup lime juice, 2 medium tomatoes, 2 dried chili peppers, 1 green pepper, sliced parsley (snipped), 1 tablespoon sugar, 2 tablespoons pimento, 1/2 teaspoon salt, clove garlic, 1/4 cup vinegar, marinate for 24 hours.

It sounded good. Too bad, like most recipes in Ellen's collection, she had never tried it. She was addicted to the same old food, the same old items. It never varied; she never varied.

Except in temperament. She thought about it. Years ago, it must have been years ago, when she had been in love with Ernesto. Ernesto was before Mario, before Manuelo. What day had she written that note? She couldn't remember. She was surprised to learn that she had been fluctuating in temperament for this many years. She had thought it was something recent, brought on by her pre-menopausal state, not that her condition was something stable like the ocean — up, down, back, forth.

On the back of the Mexican marinated fish was a recipe for baked mushrooms and barley. The recipe sounded terrible, but Ellen could remember that someone, someday, a long time ago — when she and Ernesto were living together — had brought it to a potluck. And Ellen had, at the time, thought it was tasty. Ellen wondered why she would not face facts. All the recipes she asked people for — why did she do it? Why did she delude herself? She would never fix them. They lay in the large manila folders, worn, torn, battered. And the right recipe was hard to find when she did need it. It was almost impossible to find her recipe for Caesar salad dressing, which was written on a piece of scratch paper in ink that was fading with a warning written on it: don't throw away.

Someday, Ellen told herself, she would do the things that needed to be done. She would straighten out the chaos in her life. She would move on these projects that were so overwhelming, so frightening they terrified her. Projects like digging into the recipes, like cleaning out her locker in the basement. Like reading notes on the recipes. Like seeing people's handwritings from recipes given to her long ago. People who came in and out of her life.

She thought about when she could have written that note: "I know you wonder each day we wake up together whether I will be the Beauty or the Beast." She remembered many mornings, although she could not remember this exact morning. She remembered that Ernesto would sit up in bed while she dressed for work. He would watch her dress. He would put on his glasses, stare at her. It was erotic, Ellen remembered. She would wear hose, a blouse, bra, suit, heels, earrings.

When she went over to him to kiss him goodbye, he would kiss her long and soft, his tongue moving all over her lips, teeth, mouth, ears, lobes, neck, until soon her business suit would be in a heap on the floor. She would be in bed with him. She would be late for work. This happened often, until she got fired from her job as training coordinator for a bank. She couldn't bear the thought of leaving Ernesto, but once she lost her job, she blamed him for her misfortune. He had caused it.

She really didn't love her job. She didn't approve of most of the training that she was forced to coordinate. She thought she knew best what bankers should know, but her boss disagreed. Everyone was terrified of her boss, a large woman with a nasty disposition. Her boss didn't understand how she could be so unprofessional, so unmotivated. Ellen didn't bother to explain, because she thought if this person — whom she called Lady Pigfoot — knew why Ellen was really late, she would not understand. So Ellen used other excuses. Used them up.

Ellen's friends also did not understand her fascination with Ernesto. It was not just that he knew what to do to excite her in bed; he knew plenty about that and he used every piece of knowledge he had gained God knows where. Ellen didn't want to think about where and about how many women he must have been with. She could not bear to think that there was anyone besides her. But he learned his techniques somewhere, learned them so well they didn't appear to be techniques. His lovemaking appeared to be natural, from the heart.

Ellen could not accept that. She was not ready for anyone to make a notch in her heart. She would keep her heart to herself and loan out her body. She thought there was indeed a separation between mind, body and soul, and one in fact that she had achieved.

So she stayed in bed, lost her job, went on unemployment, argued with Ernesto, blamed Ernesto, blamed herself. Now, home all day, lovemaking in the morning lost its appeal. She didn't get dressed in her business suit and he didn't get excited. Instead, she got up early, put on an old stained bathrobe, fixed a pot of coffee, perused the want-ads in the paper, which depressed her severely. Everyone said you never find any jobs in the want-ads, but Ellen kept looking.

Ernesto, once Ellen took her body away, began looking too. He didn't have to look far for women; they must have been able to smell his lust.

Maybe it would have helped if she had fixed Mexican marinated fish. Maybe she should throw out these recipes, or type them up on cards. Maybe she should do something to locate the things she wanted, the things she had lost.

Saab Story

On December 10, Ellen discovered that the bag lady had been sleeping in her car. Before that discovery, there had been telltale signs. The smell, for one. Ellen's old Saab smelled like a rat had died underneath the seat. Once Ellen had found a dead rat in the alley by her garage. It was frozen. Ellen checked on the rat daily, looked at it from a distance. Finally, she threw dead leaves and a clump of dirt on the rat so she wouldn't have to look at it anymore. Once, a neighbor in the basement apartment had found a rat in her chest of drawers. Ellen thought about rats a lot. They frightened her. She could not understand how people could watch movies about rats, movies like *Ben* and *Willard*. To Ellen, rats were scary enough. She wondered if the bag lady was afraid of rats.

In order to get the rancid smell out of her car, Ellen paid $5 to have it cleaned. If there truly was a rat under the seat, she didn't want to be the one who found it. But the guys at the car wash didn't find a dead rat under the seat. They found pennies, paper clips, dust balls, paper, broken pens.

Two other clues alerted Ellen that the bag lady was using her car. The driver's door was ajar and a package was placed on the passenger seat. It was wrapped neatly in newspaper as if it were a Christmas present. Ellen unwrapped it and found two packages of cigarettes: Virginia Slims. One package was open. Ellen tossed the package in the garbage can before she realized who it might belong to. Later, she checked the trash can to see if the package was still there. It wasn't.

Ellen knew about the bag lady. In an odd way, Ellen admired her. The bag lady managed to live without buying things she couldn't afford. The bag lady didn't measure her worth in terms of accomplishment and possessions. She was doing what most people were doing: getting by the best way she knew how. Living not on the edge, but over it.

In the summer, the bag lady had been arrested for throwing rocks at the young boys who taunted her. Ellen had learned the bag lady's name by reading it in "Police Beat." Daisy Buckman was her name. The name reminded Ellen of Daisy Buchanan from *The Great Gatsby*, F. Scott Fitzgerald's novel. This Daisy was nothing like the one in the book. In Fitzgerald's story, Daisy was soft, blonde, golden, rich. This Daisy was hard, gray, brittle, poor. Her name should have matched her looks, Ellen thought. Daisy's name should have been Maude or Beulah.

Daisy fascinated Ellen. She walked through the alley behind Ellen's apartment building smoking, muttering, cursing. The neighbors gossiped about the way she cussed, her vulgar language. Her curses frightened them — horrible words, streamed out in a cadence, a rhythm, like a poem gone bad.

Like Daisy, Ellen cursed too. A lot more than she liked. It concerned Ellen that she loved the language so much and abused it so frequently. Every New Year's she resolved to clean up her garbage mouth. But the use of the "f" word had become habitual and she used it again and again, unconsciously. Trying to stop cursing was like trying to stop smoking, Ellen thought. She had to remain conscious of her behavior and it was too much work.

From Ellen's window, she could watch Daisy cursing at people from long ago. In mild weather, she would sit at the picnic table outside the convenience store. Daisy seemed to hold conversations, shaking her finger at imaginary foes, cursing. From both her verbal and nonverbal communication, Ellen knew that Daisy was angry to the bone. In a way, Ellen envied her. At least Daisy was getting her anger outside of her now. Ellen's anger accumulated like her unpaid bills.

Daisy hung out in the garages behind Ellen's apartment building. There was a long row of them. Since Ellen had never seen Daisy in her garage in the daytime, she assumed Daisy wasn't interested in using her garage. Other neighbors had caught Daisy in their garages. One of them yelled at her, threatened her. Later, the neighbor told Ellen she didn't want Daisy in her garage. She was afraid Daisy might urinate in it. Ellen didn't worry about that. But she didn't have a new car, either. The other woman did.

If Ellen had had her dream car, an '88 Saab, she would not have liked Daisy sleeping in it, stinking up the smell of new leather. But then, if Ellen had had a new Saab, Daisy probably would not have been able to get into it. Ellen would have been able to lock the doors of her Saab. The car she now owned did not have door handles. Only the driver's side opened. To enter the car,

Ellen had to insert a long screwdriver into the hole where the handle had been and then push. Ellen kept a supply of screwdrivers in the trunk for this purpose. The trunk didn't lock either. Did Daisy know this? Had she, in fact, watched Ellen?

Ellen debated what to do about the problem. On the one hand, she worried that Daisy might oversleep and Ellen might find her in the car. She had heard that Daisy was mean, and in a way Ellen was afraid of her. Daisy was no longer in touch with reality and those kinds of people scared Ellen. Ellen had known too many people like Daisy and the effect they could have on her. Ellen felt sorry for them and they knew it.

Ellen told her kids about the bag lady using her car. Her son said once Daisy had politely asked him to bring her packets of sugar from the corner White Hen, which he did. Ellen's daughter raged. She worried that Daisy might try to get into her new car, which was occasionally parked in Ellen's garage. Ellen found herself defending Daisy, saying that she was not a thief. She would not break and enter. She would not steal. Ellen kept shoes in her back seat, good shoes. They were never missing. Ellen thought if Daisy would want to steal anything, it might be shoes. "Daisy does not steal," Ellen told her daughter. "She borrows." Still, Ellen's daughter did not relent. She accused Ellen of feeling sorry for everyone, of identifying too closely.

The truth was, Ellen worried about becoming a bag lady. She collected shopping bags from Saks Fifth Avenue, Bergdorf Goodman, Macy's. If she were to become a bag lady, she would be fashionable. She would carry the best bags in town. She wondered how many bags she would need to carry her prized possessions around with her. In the end she would probably dump them all, like Daisy, and settle for carrying a package of cigarettes in her pocket.

For Christmas, Ellen bought Daisy a package of McDonald's coupons. She wrapped the package in brightly-colored Santa Claus paper and left it on the passenger seat where she had found the cigarettes. She also left a sleeping bag in the back seat. She wondered if Daisy would cover with it.

As a Christmas present to herself, Ellen considered ordering two door handles for her Saab. She talked with her mechanic, who said they would cost about $100 apiece and that price did not include installation. Installing the door handles would be expensive, he said, because the locks were broken. It would take six weeks to get the door handles. Did she want to order them, her mechanic wanted to know. Ellen said she'd think about it.

Angel

Ellen stares at the cookies through the glass case. They are baking and smell good. There are many kinds from which to choose. Peanut butter. Chocolate chip. Macadamia nut. White chocolate. Oatmeal raisin. And her favorites — Rice Krispie squares. She takes her time, wanting to purchase something, the perfect thing to quell her hunger.

To her left, she sees a little girl crouched between the Cookie Factory and the Footlocker next door. She looks like she is about 5 years old. She looks scared.

"Are you all right?" Ellen asks softly.

The child shakes her head no and begins to cry.

"Where is your mother?" Ellen kneels down so they are at eye level.

The little girl says nothing.

"Are you at the mall with your mother?"

She nods.

"Don't cry. I'll help you find her."

Ellen can't help but notice that the child smells. A faint salty smell of sweat and unwashed hair and old clothes mingles with the smells of baking sugar, icing, muffins, bread and rising dough.

The child wears a sweater that must belong to a big brother or sister. Her pants are too short and have holes in the knees. Her shoes are scuffed and too big. She would be beautiful if she were clean, Ellen thinks. She looks like an American Indian, with long black hair that would be silky if washed.

"I have an idea," Ellen says. "Let's go upstairs to the manager's office and page your mom. The manager will announce your mother's name over the loudspeaker, and she'll hear it. Then she'll come and get you."

The little girl shakes her head.

"We can watch the people and see if we can find your mom."

The girl nods.

"What's your name?" Ellen asks.

Ellen moves closer because she cannot understand what is said in a whisper.

"Angel?"

The child nods.

"What kind of cookies do you want, Angel?"

The girl takes Ellen's hand and walks to the front of the store where the glass case displays trays of sweets. A new tray of large flat cookies with M&Ms in them are being placed in the racks. Angel points to an M&M cookie.

Ellen orders cookies for both of them and coffee for herself.

They sit on a bench under the plants and palms.

"You keep an eye out for your mom," she tells Angel. "Were the two of you alone?"

Angel shakes her head.

"Who is with your mom?"

"My grandma," Angel says softly.

"Oh. What does she look like?"

Angel shrugs.

Ellen and Angel sit under the tree eating cookies. Ellen tries to think of things that would interest a child. She has raised two children herself. She is disappointed that she cannot remember what she talked to them about when they were 5.

"When I was your age," Ellen says, "I used to play with paper dolls. And buttons. My grandma had lots of buttons. I would line them up in rows of five and play school. The big button would be the teacher and the little buttons would be the students." As Ellen talks, she watches the shoppers, thinking that she will recognize Angel's family intuitively when she sees them. She expects to see two Apaches wearing buckskins, headbands and paint.

Angel listens to the button stories. She fingers the frayed cuff of her sweater. Ellen blows on her coffee to cool it. "Some of the buttons were shiny and pretty. I liked them best. They got front-row seats. I named all of them. Pretty names. Like Pamela and Debby."

The little girl smiles, showing her blackened teeth. Ellen is upset. She wants to reprimand the mother for giving the child too many sweets, for not taking her to the dentist. Angel tugs at Ellen's sleeve and points to the coffee. She wants a drink. Ellen is appalled.

"No," Ellen says. "You must certainly not have coffee. Little girls do not drink coffee."

"I do," Angel says. "My grandma lets me have coffee. She puts milk and sugar in it."

Ellen thinks, "No wonder your teeth are rotten."

"How about some tea?" Ellen says.

Angel shakes her head no.

Ellen leaves Angel for a second while she goes into the Cookie Factory. Angel smiles when Ellen returns and gives her a cup of coffee with lots of milk in it. Ellen sits down next to Angel. She wants to take her home. She wants to teach her how to play buttons.

Ellen knows that she should contact the mall office and have them find the child's mother, but she doesn't know where the office is. She knows the bookstore and the department stores and the cookie store, but where is the office that pages parents?

"Buttons," Angel says.

"Oh yes. I would ask questions and then move the smartest buttons to the front of the room to stand by the teacher. I played buttons for hours. There were many questions. Sometimes I played for days. In the winter, I played with the Christmas tree ornaments. I'd line them up the same way and play school. The ornaments were hard to get hold of. My mom hid them. My sister and I had one that we liked the best. Her name was Bellevue. She was a shiny, light blue bell and she rang."

Angel laughs.

"My daughter spent all her time playing paper dolls. Do you play paper dolls?"

Angel nods.

"My daughter drew clothes for her paper dolls. She had more clothes than the dolls would ever wear. Then she stopped playing completely. Now she designs clothes for real people."

The shoppers are thinning out. It must be getting late. Soon the mall will close. "I'd better go to the office," Ellen says. "I have to find your mom."

Angel cries.

Ellen sits down. She looks around for help. She decides to write a note and have the young woman at the cookie counter help her call the mall office. Ellen writes what happened and describes Angel. She gives instructions for the mother to meet her at the Cookie Factory.

Ellen and Angel watch the shoppers. Angel says she plays in the yard. She likes to dig in the yard with a spoon. Digging to China. Digging for the devil. Those are games that Ellen remembers. Ellen tells Angel that she really did expect to find the devil. Angel laughs.

The loudspeaker announces that the mall will be closing soon. Ellen's message is also broadcast. She is angry at Angel's mother. How could she leave her child? Maybe it was on purpose. Maybe Angel's mother will not show up. Maybe Angel has been abandoned. Ellen will take her home. She will read books to her, refuse to give her sugar. She will buy her new clothes, play dolls, draw designer paper doll clothes. She will give her ballet lessons, educate her about Indian tribes, Apache legends. Together they will bead jewelry, practice sacred dances, pray for rain ...

Angel jumps up and runs over to the Cookie Factory. She hugs her mother. Grandma reaches down and kisses Angel's head. Ellen gathers her packages, empty cups and wrappers and walks over to where the two women stand under the yellow awning. Angel points to Ellen.

"I'm Ellen. I found your daughter here. We ate cookies while we waited for you."

"Thank you," the younger woman says meekly. "We've been looking all over for her."

Grandma interrupts. She has an accent Ellen cannot place. They look poor. The mother wears a gray cotton skirt that has been washed many times and a pink sleeveless blouse that looks like it is from the 1950s. Grandma has on men's house slippers that are patched with black electrical tape. She wears an assortment of layered clothing — wash dress, sweater and apron. Grandma holds Angel's hand. Mother says something about getting confused in the mall. She speaks so softly, Ellen can hardly hear her.

They must go. The last bus leaves soon. Ellen offers to give them a ride. They thank her but say no. Ellen hands Angel a small white bag containing extra cookies. Angel hangs onto it tightly. She walks in the middle, between Mom and Grandma. They leave. Ellen has tears in her eyes.

Hair Trigger

"I hate my hair," Ellen says to Bratley, her daughter, who lounges in the recliner.

Bratley adjusts the tea bags on her eyes. "You should go to Trish. Your hair looked good when she did it."

"Goldilocks on Xanax," Ellen says, grabbing a hunk of hair and holding it on top of her head. "Every time I go in that place I feel like I'm in an upscale crack house. The stylists match the decor. Except for Goldilocks, they all have dyed whore-black hair and white faces. It's so cold. There is no personality emanating from anyone."

"Are you paying for personality or for a haircut?" Bratley asks, pressing lightly on the tea bags. "I hope these work. My eyes are so puffy."

"Trish doesn't even know who I am and she's cutting my hair. Every time I go in, she asks how the real estate business is. Every time, I tell her I don't sell real estate. Every time, she says, 'Oh, what do you do?' I relish the lies I could tell her. 'I search for good haircuts,' I want to say. 'I'm like John Wayne in *The Searchers*. I won't give up until I get results, until I find what I'm looking for: one haircut that can grow out without me being aware of it.' In all my years of haircuts, I've only had one like that."

Bratley sips tea. "I know. Stephen from Vidal Sasson who used to be in Chicago. So go to Minnesota and get your hair cut."

Ellen lies back on the sofa. "I'll never forget the day he cut my hair. He stood, sweater tied around his shoulders, and cut my hair while every stylist watched. He made it look so easy. I felt like I was in the hands of a true professional."

"That was a good haircut," Bratley agrees. She takes the tea bags off her eyes to look through *Vogue*. "They have a really good article in here about Fragile X Syndrome," she says.

"I hate reading about chromosomes," Ellen says. "I can never figure out how so many of us turned out normal. It's so scary."

"You should read this one, though. It's really interesting. Isn't that what the doctor thought was wrong with Stafford?"

"Yes," Ellen says, releasing the clump of hair she has been holding off her face. "But that's not what the chromosome studies showed. He has tags on his chromosomes, extra pieces." She pauses. "Don't forget to get an amniocentesis before your fourth month if you ever get pregnant," she warns Bratley.

"I'm on the pill, remember. I can't get pregnant." Bratley flashes her black eyes at Ellen. Ellen thinks Bratley could have added "stupid" on the end of the sentence.

Bratley reads and Ellen thinks about all the haircuts and hair colors she has tried in her lifetime. She talks out loud, more to herself than to Bratley, who is reading about two of her favorite people: Christy Turlington and Linda Evangelista. Ellen knows their names but wouldn't recognize their faces. Bratley knows everything, including the size of their thighs.

"After I graduated from high school, before I married your dad, I used to get my hair done by a girl I went to high school with — Sarah Simpson. She had a surly little sister who used to wash the customers' hair. Sarah told us one of her customers didn't have a left ear. Just a hole where an ear should have been."

"That's gross," Bratley says, flipping through the ads in the magazine.

"I was complaining because my ears were too big. Then I felt bad." Ellen thinks about Sarah Simpson, who sells real estate in New York, her sister Tana, who died of ovarian cancer, and her mother, who was stabbed by her lover after she left a bar one night.

The phone rings. Bratley answers.

"What's up," she says to the voice at the other end.

While Bratley talks on the phone, Ellen thinks about how Sarah used to rat and spray her hair, sculpting it into a beehive. It lasted for a week. Ellen had to scratch her scalp with a knitting needle. At night, she wrapped the hairdo in toilet paper. Once the toilet paper slipped down over Ellen's eyes. When she woke up, she couldn't see. She thought she had been stricken blind. She figured she would go blind because that would be the worst thing that could happen to a person. At that time, Ellen didn't know about extra, or not enough, chromosomes.

"That was Jill," Bratley says. "We're going to work out at the Club. Have you seen my sweats? You didn't let Stafford wear them, did you?"

Ellen shakes her head.

"Maybe I will go back to Trish. It's just a haircut."

"You need to get it tinted, too. Your roots are showing." Bratley starts to leave the room. "And please do something about those hairs on your chin and neck. They are disgusting."

Bratley leaves and returns with a shiny black mirror.

Ellen starts to get up. "Stay right where you are," Bratley orders. "Natural light is the best light you can have." She thrusts the mirror at Ellen.

Ellen sees roots and wrinkles. Large hairs protrude from her chin and neck.

"You're right," she tells Bratley. "My entire face is one big wrinkle. My face is sagging. And these hairs are enormous."

"I told you," Bratley says. "Your face isn't that bad. It's not as bad as Jill's mother's neck. Now that is nauseating. Chicken neck ... ugh."

"I've never noticed," Ellen says. Bratley rolls her eyes. She takes the mirror from Ellen and checks her own face.

"The tea bags didn't work," she says. "Do we have any cucumbers?"

Joanne Throws a Party

I had never had a birthday party. One of my sisters had had one once. She used to tell me about it. Guests had come. They'd brought presents. There'd been a cake. Ice cream too, and candles that she blew out.

I dreamed sometimes about having a birthday party like my sister Joanne's. I was wearing a white striped eyelet pinafore and white anklets and black patent leather shoes, and my hair was long and curly. That was in the dream, because my hair was straight. And I got presents. Lots of them.

I asked my mother once why I couldn't have a birthday party. "We don't have the money, honey," she said. "The welfare check doesn't come till the end of the month, and it never covers everything it has to. Look at you. You need new shoes. They were Joanne's, and now they're too little for you. They're hurting your feet. How can I buy presents and cake when you need new shoes?"

"I'll go barefoot," I said, but Mother laughed and shook her head.

Then something wonderful happened. My sister knew I wanted a birthday party. She knew I dreamed about it. She knew I wanted a little gold locket in the dime store; I'd shown it to her. "Rosie," she said, "I'm going to give you a birthday party. Invite your friends."

I invited my friends. Sandy and Rena and Loren and Charlotte and Penny. Joanne told me to tell them to come at 1 o'clock on Saturday, so that's what I told them. And they came.

But before that, in the morning, I watched Joanne bake the cake. Chocolate with white marshmallow icing. She had ice cream, too. It was next door in Mrs. Harrison's refrigerator; she had a freezer section. Mrs. Harrison had a telephone, too. She let us use it. She also had a fat husband who had only one leg, and he used to sit in a porch swing in the yard with his one leg up and the stump hanging, and smile. But that hasn't got anything to do with the birthday party.

Mother was at work. Grandma was at home, but we were left pretty much by ourselves because Grandma used to lock herself in her room with her schmattes, which means old rags. She embroidered them. They weren't all old rags; some were new dishtowels, but they were mostly old rags. Her room was full of them.

Joanne and her friend Janet, who lived three units down, left right after Joanne finished icing the cake. They were going to town. Joanne said she was going to buy me a present. She said, "Don't you dare start that party till I get back." Just because it was my birthday and she was giving me a party didn't mean she had to be nice to me too.

Joanne was big. And mean and tough. She wasn't afraid of anything or anybody. Mother was afraid of her. Grandma and Joanne, though, were probably evenly matched. Grandma was mean too. Judy was my other sister. She was older than Joanne and she was never home. They hated each other. Grandma hated Judy because she looked like my dad. She spit in her face lots of times, Judy told me later, but Grandma was nice to me. I was the baby, and that's what she called me. Baby, and Faygala. Means "little bird." She said it did. She embarrassed me to death, going out in the neighborhood, calling, "Faygala, Faygala, come home, Faygala!" The other kids would call me Faygala and I'd just die.

Grandma and Joanne got along fine. They respected each other's meanness. But I keep getting off the birthday party.

I watched the cake. I didn't dare touch it, but I wanted it real bad. I was so excited — the thought of actually getting a birthday present, a new something, a new anything, was almost more than I could bear. I just sat and thought about what present Joanne was going to bring home to me and what it would feel like to open it and have something somebody had bought for you that was going to be all your own. We didn't pray at our house, but I sometimes prayed secretly, and that was one of the times I really prayed. I created a picture in my mind of that little gold heart-shaped locket, and I prayed.

My friends came down. They didn't bring presents, but that was all right. I knew they wouldn't. Their moms didn't have any money either. It was enough that Joanne was getting me a present. Sandy did bring me a pen, but she'd given me one once before. Her dad worked for state fairs; he followed them around from state to state. He had all kinds of junk. We found it exciting.

Once I stayed overnight with Sandy. It was the first time I'd ever been overnight in a house with a man. He came home drunk, late at night, and he beat up Sandy's mother. I lay on the bunk bed and just shook all over, I was so scared. I thought he might come up the stairs and beat Sandy and me too. Sandy had told me that sometimes, if they were up, he beat them too. But he didn't come up, and I didn't stay at Sandy's again. But I am away from the birthday party.

They all came at 1 o'clock. Sandy and Loren and Rena and Charlotte and Penny. Grandma was in her room. We looked at the cake. Nobody dared touch it. They all were afraid of Joanne too. We waited for Joanne and Janet to get back.

We waited.
We waited.
We waited.
We waited.
It got to be 2 o'clock.
It got to be 2:30.
It got to be 3 o'clock.

I was sure she had forgotten all about the party. She'd gone to town and probably gone to a movie instead with the money for my present. I was mad. I was hurt. Disappointed. I was embarrassed. I was supposed to be having a birthday party and my friends were here, waiting. We could see the cake and we couldn't touch it. There weren't any games. Oh, we tried drop the clothespins in the bottle, but I was too upset to get into the spirit.

Deep down, I trusted Joanne, though. She wouldn't do that to me, not on this day. She was as excited about throwing the party as I was about having it. Mom always said, "Joanne has a good heart," and deep down I knew that. So I began to worry that something might have happened.

And then she came. She burst in the door and said, "Shit, man, me and Janet just found a dead man! By the tracks!" Janet was right behind her.

We crowded around, and they told us about it. They'd been coming back from the dime store, and they'd jumped over the cement wall by Producers Dairy and there, laid up against the wall by the tracks, was a dead man with blood on him.

"Just plopped against the wall," Joanne kept saying. "We didn't know whether he was sick or dead, but he wasn't breathing and his eyes were rolled back and all open, and we were scared."

It took a lot to scare Joanne. We were all petrified, just listening to her. We could see, she told it so well.

"We started to run, and as we were running down the tracks, there were these two men coming. They were wearing hats. They yelled at us, 'Hey, you kids!' We turned around and ran the other way, back past the dead man, and over the wall, and we hid until it was safe and the men in the hats were gone."

The birthday party was forgotten. The locket was forgotten. We wanted to see the dead man too, not just in our heads the way Joanne told it. "Take us back there! Take us with you!" we cried, because we knew Joanne was going to go back.

So Joanne took us with her. All the way, we kept a lookout for the men with the hats. We got to the wall, crept up to it and peeked over. The dead man was gone.

Joanne was mad. She thought we'd think she'd been lying, because she did lie, lots.

"He's not there," she said, "But look. Here's the blood where he was."

We all climbed over and stared at the blood-stained wall. It was even still wet, in a crack at the bottom. We believed her.

"Shit," said Joanne. "Let's go home and eat the cake."

So we did. We got the ice cream from Mrs. Harrison's refrigerator. A couple of the kids were still mad because they couldn't see the dead man. But really, I think we were all glad because he wasn't there, just the bloodstains that meant he had been. And they didn't stay mad, because we had cake and ice cream, and there were eight candles, and I blew them all out except one with my first blow.

Then came the time for the present.

"Shit," said Joanne. "What'd I do with it?"

I started to cry. "You didn't lose it!"

"Hell no. I wrapped it and everything."

I told you Joanne was tough.

"It's gotta be around here somewhere. I threw it when I came in the door to tell you about the dead man."

We all started hunting. I was the one who found it. It was underneath the couch. It was all wrapped, in pink and white and silver flowered paper. It had a white curly bow on it, the kind you curl with the scissors. I wanted to open it, but I didn't want to open it. I wanted to just look at it, my first present ever. But of course I couldn't do that, because the kids were all crowded around me waiting, and Joanne was too.

So I opened it.

It was the golden locket. The prettiest locket in the whole world. Heart-shaped, on a little chain, and it lay in a little box with red velvet backing.

I cried.

That was my first present, and my only birthday party. I didn't have a white eyelet pinafore and I didn't have white anklets with no holes, and black patent leather shoes. There weren't lots and lots of presents, and my hair never did curl. I don't know to this day where Joanne got the money for the cake mix or the candles or the locket. Maybe she charged the cake mix on our food bill down at the corner grocery. Maybe she shoplifted the locket. I don't care. I do know it was the best birthday party anyone ever had, and I loved the locket, and I loved Joanne.

After that, none of us ever went past that wall without seeing the dead man there, and the two men with the hats. Janet says she dreams about him still.

Christmas Cake

That Christmas, everyone forgave everyone in our house. Grandma forgave Alana. Alana forgave Joe. Joe forgave me. And Mom forgave all of us.

At first, Grandma wasn't sure she should forgive Alana. She wanted to know what the Bible said about forgiveness. Specifically, she wanted to know how many times she should forgive. Grandma had never read the Bible, but she had read the Torah. Mom had read the Bible and the Torah. Alana was taking a Bible study course at Third Presbyterian Church. She wanted to teach Sunday school. Sometimes I went to church with Alana and her boyfriend William. Joe was going to St. Vincent de Paul because his girlfriend Mary Jean was going there. Joe had a lot of girlfriends — they lasted about a month. I went to Mass with him and Mary Jean. Grandma went to Temple Israel. I tagged along with her, too. Mom stayed home and watched Billy Graham and Oral Roberts on TV.

I liked how churches felt inside. They all felt the same, kind of like the library. A quiet place to pray without the smells of everyday life. Churches didn't feel used like houses.

Anyway, that Christmas, Grandma kept asking me and Joe if she should forgive Alana. Joe ignored the question. I tried to figure out the correct answer. What did the Bible say about forgiveness? Was it, Grandma wanted to know, to forgive seven times, or seven times seven, or seventy times seven?

Christmas Eve morning, Grandma baked rolls and bread. She gave me an apron to wear, and we got flour all over while she pinched and kneaded and rolled the dough on the breadboard. Using her hands, she sprinkled sugar and flour in a wooden bowl. She pinched in small touches of baking powder and salt. After the dough was mixed, Grandma covered the bowl with a dishtowel and let the bread rise for two hours. While the dough rose, she prayed at the window. Looking upward, she rocked back and forth and chanted. I sat quietly, making designs in leftover flour and rolling remnants of dough into balls. Later, Grandma pressed out flat, round globs of dough with a jelly glass. She added cinnamon, nuts, apples and sugar and wrapped the edges of the dough together.

"Should I forgive her, mine Angel?" She called me "Angel" and "Faygala," but my real name is Ellen.

"Yes," I told Grandma. "Forgive her."

Her eyes told me she believed what I was saying.

"You should forgive Alana because Joe forgave me," I told Grandma.

"Nu, why should he be mad at you? You do not hurt him?" She put the rolls on a baking sheet.

"Yes, I did. I broke all his model airplanes. He was really mad. But he said he forgave me. And he even said he would get me a Christmas present."

Grandma threw up her hands. "Presents," she said. "Oy gevalt."

"Alana forgave Joe," I told Grandma. "He read all her love letters from William. She was really mad. But I heard her tell Mom that she was getting Joe a present." I stuck my finger in the leftover cinnamon and tasted it.

"Love letters?" Grandma muttered "goyim" under her breath.

"Mom said she forgave all of us for acting like idjits. She said she's working hard to make ends meet, and she doesn't want us fighting all the time." I tried to picture ends meeting, a phrase Mom used often that I thought I understood.

I wondered if Mom would ever forgive Grandma for not forgiving Alana. Not that Alana had ever done anything to forgive. All she had done was resemble our dad, who was, according to Grandma, "a gentile."

I didn't remember much about Dad. Mom said he was a good man, but he lived too far away to come see us. Joe said he was a rat, and he was glad Dad left. Alana kept a picture of him on her dresser, but she kept her bedroom door locked so Grandma wouldn't destroy it. Grandma said Dad was a bum who hit her once and hit Mom too. I remembered, vaguely, a fight and a suitcase and nothing else.

Grandma said Alana looked just like him. In a family where everyone had dark hair and large noses, Alana's green eyes and small nose stood out. Her eyes sparkled like tree lights. Her skin glowed pink, like a cherub's. Her nose was perfect — it turned up just a little at the end. Once, Alana sang "Has Anybody Seen My Gal" on the radio after Thanksgiving and won $100.

"Like a shiksa," Grandma said that night when we sat around the kitchen table listening to the radio. When she said those words, it sounded like she was spitting.

Mom beat her fist on the table. "Don't you dare talk about her like that," she yelled at Grandma. "If you say one more nasty word about her, you can go live with Aunt Sarah. I won't have my daughter treated this way."

"Should I forgive her?" Grandma asked. The line repeated itself like a chorus from a Christmas carol. "Should I forgive mine enemies?"

Grandma stuffed the turkey and put it in the oven. While she cleaned up the kitchen, she let me wrap money for the Christmas cake. Every Christmas Eve, Grandma baked a money cake. Usually, she used half-dollars, quarters and dimes. Once, I found a silver dollar, wrapped tightly in waxed paper, in my piece of cake.

While Grandma mixed the eggs, flour and sugar, I curled up in the mohair chair beside the Christmas tree and wrote a story. Every winter story had the same beginning: "It was a cold, snowy night as Angel walked down the street." From there, Angel met new friends and went exploring. They crossed the tracks and looked into an old house where a witch lived. In the end, they were chased home by the witch and ended up in the snow, making snow angels. Then they made hot chocolate with whipped cream on top and played Monopoly.

In the summer, the opening to the story varied: "It was a sunny day as Angel walked down the street." She would still have adventures, but instead of making snow angels, they would get under the sprinkler.

From the kitchen, Grandma talked steadily as she baked. I had heard the story before. How she came over on a big, big boat from Rooshia. She talked about soldiers at the door with guns, about her sister Passey, whom she never saw again. At this point in the story, she cried. I usually did too, but not tonight. Tonight the tree lights were on. The turkey was in the oven.

About 6 o'clock, the door opened and Joe walked in carrying a big dog in his arms. "Damn, it's cold out there," he said, bending down to let the dog onto the floor.

"A dog! Is she ours? Can we keep her? Is this my present?"

"Sure is," Joe said. He shook the snow off his boots and his leather jacket. He lit a cigarette. "Get a towel for me, will you? I want to dry her off." I ran upstairs and got Mom's best towel.

"She's been hanging around the station," Joe said. "Pitiful thing. I thought she needed to get warm. She looks half frozen."

Joe rubbed the dog with the towel. Grandma stood by, watching. Grandma hated dogs, but she loved Joe, so she didn't tell him to take the dog out.

"Joey, Joey," Grandma said. It sounded like "Jewy."

"Hey, Grandma. How ya doing? Baking your famous rolls, I bet. I could smell them all the way down at the station. Are they done yet?"

"He likes mine biscuits," Grandma said to me, smiling.

"Everybody likes your biscuits," I said. I knelt down with Joe and helped him dry the dog.

"What's her name?" I asked. The dog looked at me with sad eyes. She was shivering.

"Noel. We'll call her Nolie for short. How's that? A Christmas dog with a Christmas name." Joe rubbed the dog's head. "Like that, Nolie?"

"Nolie," I repeated softly. I wondered how a beautiful name like Noel could be turned into something as casual as Nolie.

"Mine Sarahala. Will she come tonight?" Grandma asked Joe.

"Sure," Joe said. "Aunt Sarah and Uncle Phil always come by on Christmas Eve. They'll be here."

Grandma rubbed her floured hands on her apron. "Mine Sarahala. Ohhh — I cannot wait to look on her."

Joe sat down at the piano. He lit another cigarette. The dog crawled next to the wall by the piano and lay down on the heat register. "What do you want to hear, Angel?" Joe blew a smoke ring in the air, then put his cigarette in the ash tray.

"Deck the halls with boughs of holly," I sang.

Joe played; I sang. Grandma checked the turkey and the cake. The dog slept.

"Grandma," Joe yelled into the kitchen. "Bring me some Mogen David."

Grandma rushed into the living room, a bottle of Mogen David in one hand and two small jelly glasses in the other. "One holiday drink, nu?" She poured two glasses of wine and sat on the piano bench with Joe.

Joe played "Jingle Bells."

The back door opened and Mom and Alana came in. They carried large brown paper bags filled with packages. As Alana entered the kitchen, Grandma backed out.

"Santa's here," Joe said. "Time to open presents."

"Santa doesn't come in the back door," I told Joe. "It's just Mom and Alana."

"You can't look yet," Alana warned. "We still have a few presents to wrap." She went into the back room.

I ran to Mom and hugged her. She smelled like cold and perfume. I could feel her shaking.

"My little Angel," she said. "Are you having fun with Joe? Is that a dog in the living room?"

"Joe brought her home. Oh, it was so cold, Mom. You should have seen her. Joe said she would freeze outside. Can we keep her? She's so cute. Joe calls her Nolie — for Noel. Please, Mom."

"We'll see," Mom said. "I have to help Alana right now. You stay with Joe and Grandma."

"Please, Mom. She's so cute. We've got to keep her."

Grandma got the turkey ready and set the table for dinner. After we ate turkey, potatoes and cranberries, we went into the living room and sat around the tree. Alana put a Christmas album on the stereo. She had dressed up to go out with William, and she looked like the Christmas angel on top of the tree. Her face glowed, and she wore a blue velvet dress that she had made herself. It was trimmed in white fur and had a low-cut neckline. She looked glamorous, I thought, like one of my paper dolls. Her golden hair shone.

"You look like the angel on our tree," I told Alana, pointing upward to the top.

"You just want two presents instead of one, huh," Alana said.

"No, I really mean it. You look so pretty. I love that dress."

Alana tugged on her hem. "It's not right. I didn't put the zipper in right and it feels funny."

"You can't tell, dear," Mom said. "You look like a princess."

"She is a princess, isn't she?" Joe said. "At least she thinks she is."

"Don't start, Joe. It's Christmas Eve. Be nice to Alana, and she'll be nice to you," Mom said.

"Don't worry about me," Alana said. "I'm leaving soon. William's coming at 9." Alana looked into the mirror that hung above the radio and checked her makeup. "I wish I looked like Aunt Sarah. She is so pretty. She looks like Ava Gardner." Alana sighed. "Oh well, let's open presents."

Mom gave me a doll for my collection. Joe gave me a set of Blue Waltz perfume and powder. Alana bought me a pair of blue jeans lined in blue plaid flannel.

Mom got a Harry Belafonte album from Alana, which she said she loved. Alana got Joe two 45s: "Don't Be Cruel" by Elvis Presley and "Blue Suede Shoes" by Carl Perkins. Mom got Joe a sweater and socks. Alana asked me to hand Grandma's present to her. I knew she was afraid to do it, so I did. Grandma opened a velvet box that had a brooch in it. Grandma was thrilled. She thought the red cut-glass stones were rubies. From across the room, Grandma thanked Alana. Alana forced a smile.

"Hello," bellowed Uncle Phil as he and Aunt Sarah came in the back door. "Happy Hanukkah."

Uncle Phil carried a shopping bag filled with presents and a mesh bag full of oranges. He and Aunt Sarah came from Chicago.

"Mine Sarahala," Grandma cried as she hugged Aunt Sarah.

"What about me?" Uncle Phil reminded Grandma. "Doesn't your son-in-law get a hug too?"

Grandma squeezed his hand.

Aunt Sarah passed out packages to everyone. They were wrapped in gold paper and had pretty red ribbons on them, the kind you curl with the scissors. I opened mine and found a scarf and gloves.

"So how's the car business?" Uncle Phil asked Joe.

Joe shrugged. "It's a job," he said. "I'm learning a lot. One of these days, I'll be driving a DeSoto like yours, Uncle Phil."

"That should happen to you, Joseph. You should have a car like mine one of these days. That would be a good thing." Uncle Phil nodded his head up and down.

"You could take your mother shopping," Aunt Sarah said. "The poor dear has to take the bus." Aunt Sarah looked at Mom and patted her hand.

"I like taking the bus, Sarah. It keeps me thin." Mom patted Aunt Sarah's arm.

"Too thin, if you ask me," Aunt Sarah said. "She eats like a bird," she said to Uncle Phil.

"Let's have presents again," Uncle Phil said. "Here's two that aren't opened." He handed them to Grandma, who tore the wrapping off and found a bottle of Peppermint Schnapps. Grandma gave Phil a sloppy kiss on the cheek, which he wiped off. Next, she opened a carton of Luckies.

"Play Mom's new record," I said.

Alana put it on the record player. Harry Belafonte belted out "Jamaica Farewell" and Uncle Phil began to cha-cha. He grabbed Alana's hand. "I'm dancing with a movie star," he said, smiling at Aunt Sarah.

"Joseph, you should learn to dance. The ladies love men who can dance." Uncle Phil winked at me, while he twirled Alana around by his side.

Alana protested. "I don't know these steps," she said.

"Joe knows how to dance," I told Uncle Phil. "He taught me the lindy. He dances good like you, Uncle Phil."

"Is this true? Joe, you must dance for us. This we have to see."

Joe got up from the piano and began to cha-cha. He held one hand to his stomach and one in the air. Uncle Phil clapped.

"So who's Mary Jean?" Aunt Sarah asked. "Is this the one?"

"It's the one this week," Alana said. "It's a different one every week for this Casanova." Alana stopped cha-chaing to answer the phone, which was in the kitchen. Grandma's cake sat on the table and Alana dipped her finger in the icing.

"Don't eat mine icing," Grandma yelled. "I want that cake should go with the coffee!" Alana's hand dropped quickly.

"Teach me to cha-cha," I begged Uncle Phil. I tugged at his sleeve.

Uncle Phil held my hand and called out the steps. "Forward two, three, four and back two, three, four. That's it, Angel. You're a natural."

I cha-chaed with Uncle Phil. Joe cha-chaed with Alana. I heard Alana admonish Joe about the dog. Dog smells and dog hair.

"You'll never notice," Joe said to Alana. "You're never home."

Aunt Sarah and Mom cha-chaed together. Grandma sat on the piano bench and smoked Lucky Strikes and drank Peppermint Schnapps.

"Come on, Mom," Aunt Sarah said. "Come cha-cha with us."

"No cha-cha," Grandma said, shaking her head. "Only dance black bottom."

The tree lights glowed. I brought in the cake. The sour cream icing was smeared, and the cake was lopsided and broken, jagged like a fault line.

"It's Jesus's birthday. Can we light candles and sing?"

"Naw," Joe said. "Jews don't celebrate the birth of Jesus."

"I can sing Happy Hanukkah for you. Joe, can you play it?" Uncle Phil tousled Joe's hair.

"I don't know it," Joe said. "But I sure know I want some of Grandma's cake. I want to find that silver dollar again."

"Joey likes mine cake," Grandma bragged to Uncle Phil. "Every day he says, 'Grandma, bake for me something sweet.'"

Grandma and Aunt Sarah got plates and cups. We sat in the living room. I had coffee with lots of cream and sugar. Uncle Phil found a $5 bill in his mouth and pushed it out. "Five dollars!" I yelled. "Grandma, you never put $5 in before."

Everyone laughed. Alana said it was a joke and that Uncle Phil put his own money in his mouth just for fun. Uncle Phil said he found it in the cake, but Grandma was laughing so much I knew it must be a joke.

After the cake, we danced until Alana left with William. Joe went over to Mary Jean's to go to midnight Mass. Aunt Sarah and

Uncle Phil went to stay with friends. Mom read *True Confessions* and fell asleep on the couch. Grandma and I cleaned up the dishes. I ate Alana's cake, which she hadn't touched.

"Look on me," Grandma said. "See mine rubies." She pointed to the brooch Alana had given her. "Tonight I forgive Alana," she said. "I forgive mine enemies. This is good, no?"

"Yes, it is good, Grandma. It's what Christmas is about."

Love to Larry
8/20/44 - 7/21/87

Every Valentine's Day I think about you. In 1962, you delivered a telegram to me in French class at Lanphier High School. You were serious that day — at least for the five minutes it took you to enter the class, approach the much-feared French teacher and hand the telegram to her. As you walked out the door, you smirked and whispered: *scada root.* I can't recall why those words were supposed to be funny, but all of us laughed every time you said them.

Furlich, our French teacher, called my name in class after you left. She had made us take French names and while most students feared her, I respected her. She had given me a new identity. "Françoise," she said, "you have a telegram." Françoise was less confusing than my other nicknames: Angel, Apache, Faygala. I could be Françoise.

It took me a while to figure out your telegram, also written in French. I had not expected romance from you, since the beauty of our relationship was that we laughed together. A couple of times we dated, but it was never like any other "date" I had ever had.

The valentine said (in French), "You are pretty, true and fair. It's too bad you aren't my mother." I laughed as soon as I understood that the message wasn't about love or commitment.

Once, when you had broken up with Bev and I had broken up with Ray, we went out together. We had two dates that I remember and we never did anything date-like; we never kissed. The first date was after a football game, and you wore your lion's mascot outfit. We went out for chili.

Afterward we went back to Val's, where I was living at the time. Her mother had a dress shop in the apartment building on North Grand and we danced in front of the three-way mirror, showing our colors. I was wearing my favorite outfit: an orange plaid wool poncho, which I was modeling for Val's mom Pearl, and my orange Capezios. You were wearing the lion's suit. We listened to the radio and danced to the Tokens singing "The Lion Sleeps Tonight." Ah weem a wet, ah weem a wet.

At one point, you put on the lion's head and I laughed so hard that I began passing wind and couldn't stop. We rolled on the polished hardwood floors, caught in a laughing fit and trying to be quiet so we wouldn't wake Pearl.

I thought I would never be able to look you in the face again, after that. Sixteen-year-old girls don't usually fart on dates and live to tell about it. But the next time you saw me, you just said the three-letter word you always used that told the story: "Kid," you said. And we started laughing again.

I never ate chili again on a date. Experience is the best teacher, someone once said, and sometimes the only.

The second date we had was after high school when the fun was over and we were trying to face reality. There were no noon dances in the 9-to-5 world, we learned. I was filing checks in the basement of a downtown bank; you were off to become a fireman — a career well-suited to you since most of your senior year was spent chasing ambulances, fire engines and police cars.

This time we had again broken up with our partners. I had broken my engagement. We were both free for about one week. During that time, we went to an invite and danced to Billy Wade and the Blue Devils at the Elks Club. I had purchased a black crepe dress for the occasion. When I bought it, I didn't really expect to dance in it. I had planned to go with my fiance, who would only dance slow. But we danced every dance with abandon. When at last the night was through, we stood outside the Elks Club on Sixth Street and you said, "Kid, your dress shrunk."

Indeed it had. We had perspired and my dress was much smaller. We laughed so hard we could hardly find our way to your car. When we finally got to my house, we sat on the porch steps in the hot July night and laughed some more. About that time, my fiance drove up and asked you if he could talk to me. He was big and you were scared, you said later. You left. He stayed.

Every once in a while, I would run into you at Sangamon State University in the early '80s. You were studying labor relations and caught up in city politics. I was immersed in women's studies and the plight of women in general. We would speak, ask about other classmates, give regards to families. But I always wanted to say, "Want to go out for chili?"

Maybe I should have sent a telegram ... in French.

The Screening Committee

Dick looked good at work. He wore a three-piece suit. He was tall. His eyes were pretty, although a little mistrusting. He seemed fairly pleasant, almost gentle, yet confused. There was something about Dick that Jane just couldn't put her finger on.

Dick stared at Jane often. The place where they worked was impersonal, so any contact they had seemed almost intimate.

Sometimes they had coffee together. Dick was married. Unhappily, of course. The only reason Jane had been even remotely interested in Dick was that he had been pegged by her office workers as "eligible." Dick saw himself as semi-eligible. Jane saw herself as semi-eligible.

One day Dick asked Jane if she would take him to a bar that he had heard about, but never been to. He did not drive. That struck Jane as fairly odd; she didn't know exactly why. His vision was not good, he said, which clearly indicated there was a problem. A stick in the eye when he was young.

But, back to the date. The name of the bar was the Stopped Clock, and Jane had reservations about going there. Her new, recently acquired main man showed up there often and she was not eager to run into him while she was with another man, lest he think she was either promiscuous or flighty or any of the other bad names given to women who fuck for the sake of fucking.

Jane wasn't quite sure how she felt about going out with Dick when the time came. First of all, she had gotten new stereo equipment, had been without a "box" since her February rip-off. Jane had waited a long time to listen to her albums. She was anxious to hear Billie Holiday belt out her rendition of "I Can't Pretend," longed for the thrill of Bessie Smith's "Kitchen Man," wanted to exercise to Manu Dibango's *Soul Makossa* album, to relax to Herbie Mann, and she felt she couldn't wait another day to have her battery recharged and her mind rejuvenated from sweet and powerful Chris Williamson. So she put off calling Dick until 8 o'clock; she had said she would call him at 7.

His line was busy. Jane called again.

Dick answered.

"Have you been trying to call?" he asked.

"Yes," she admitted.

"I've been talking to a friend. She has some problems. I've been giving her some advice."

"Oh, the T.A., counselor in action," Jane teased.

"Yes, in a way. I feel really sorry for my friend. She has three children and has remarried. The man she married is several years younger than her. He's never had children before, and she can't have any and she's pretty upset. His brother's wife is pregnant and it's pretty rough on her." Dick sounded genuinely concerned.

"I can't understand why any woman would want more children when she already has three," snapped Jane. "God, who'd want to go through that process again, rug rats and the whole scene. I just can't imagine."

Dick was silent.

Jane realized that she sounded like a bitter bitch, so she lightened up a little and tried unsuccessfully to add a flippant, "But I guess if you're in love ..."

They made plans to go out.

Jane picked up Dick for their big date. They arrived at the Stopped Clock about 9 o'clock. Jane was feeling peculiar. The bar was full of younger people, people she knew, people she wanted to talk with, and there was something about Dick that just didn't fit in. Jane was a great one for fits. She liked for things and people and situations to fit. This clearly was not fitting.

Dick ordered a beer, and another and another and another. Jane ordered Jack Daniels on the rocks — one. Jane breathed a sigh of relief when she saw that her main man hadn't shown up.

With each sip of Jack, Dick began to look more strange. Jane was glad she hadn't gotten stoned. The situation would be unbearable. Jane just sat and looked and stared and talked to all her friends as they walked by and waved. Jane wished she was alone. Dick seemed fairly content. He liked the antiques in the bar and the beer.

Jane spent considerable time watching the door and hoping Michael would not arrive. But as she sipped and watched, he entered.

He walked in and Jane turned her head and pretended not to see him and hoped he might do the same. He walked the length of the bar and then back. On his way back, he stopped and smiled at Jane.

"I thought that was your car outside," he said.

"Yes, it is." Jane looked into his eyes and couldn't say anything else. She wanted to say a whole bunch of things at once. Thoughts flitted through her mind and almost out of her mouth, which she had clamped conspicuously shut. Could she say, "God, I'm just dying to talk to you, but this bozo on the barstool next to me is my date." No, no, she couldn't say that. Maybe whisper, "Look, I can't talk now, but I really have got to talk to you."

Michael got the drift of her silence and went to sit down at a table by the door. Jane sat with Dick, not speaking and hating him for nothing in particular, just everything in general. Dick smoked cigarettes and drank beer and liked the bar. Jane stared at Michael and guzzled Jack Daniels and wished one of them was somewhere else.

After what seemed like hours, Jane suggested that they leave. To get out of the bar, they had to walk right past Michael; he didn't look up. Jane felt terrible. It was awful and she didn't know why. She had only just met Michael. They had no ties, no agreements, no commitments. They had only shared sexual erotica. Why did she care who he saw her with? Why did she feel the need to explain what was going on?

Once outside the bar in the hot night air, Jane said, "God, I'm glad to be out of there. The man I'm seeing was in there and it made me feel uncomfortable." It was out. Now she should feel better.

"Why didn't you say something? We could have left sooner," Dick said in a patronizing voice, wearing a patronizing smile and opening the car door for her.

Why didn't I say something sooner, Jane wondered. It irritated her that he opened the car door for her.

"Yeah, I guess I should have," Jane mumbled. "What do you want to do now?"

"Let's go dancing," Dick said smoothly, with a hint of anxiety showing.

Let's go home, Jane thought. Separately.

Jane drove to the dance place.

He suggested a spot where she could park.

She suggested that she would park where she damn well pleased.

They parked and got out of the car. He took her arm.

They sat down at a table in the disco place, not speaking to one another.

Dick spent most of his time smiling at Jane. Jane spent most of her time looking at the plastic plants and wondering why anyone would use plastic plants in their very own establishment.

When Jane wasn't looking at the plants, she was watching the dancers or smiling back at Dick. When the waiter came to take their order, Dick said, "Are you going to order that hard stuff again or do you want something lighter?" He was smiling.

"Lighter," Jane answered almost automatically. Maybe she'd feel better in the morning with something lighter, although she wasn't at all sure there was anything wrong with Jack Daniels. Hell, she rarely drank, and she was a Leo. When she did anything, she liked drama and flair. Jack gave her that.

Dick didn't.

Dick smiled.

Dick and Jane smiled.

See the couple. They are very nice. Smile, couple, smile.

Death and Jane

Jane drives down the highway in her 1970 maroon LTD. A hitchhiker is standing at the side of the road. Jane pulls over and stops.

"Hop in," she motions.

The person hops in, slams the door and settles in.

"Been waiting long for a ride?" Jane asks, eager to start conversation. She is nervous and strung out from driving.

"Not too long. I've been waiting for you. I knew you'd come along."

Jane stares at the person briefly. He reaches over and grabs the steering wheel. The car begins to veer back and forth. Jane fights to gain control of the wheel.

"What are you trying to do?" she cries. "Kill me? Who are you? How do you know me?"

"I'm Death," he answers. "Here, have one of my calling cards."

Death hands Jane a calling card.

"Where did you have these printed up?" Jane asks. "Good print job. I like it. It's unusual — ebony and ivory. Must have been expensive."

"They were expensive. But in my business, nothing is too good for my customers."

"Far out. But leave your hands off my steering wheel. I have enough trouble driving without you interfering."

"I can't leave you alone. Don't you remember meeting me last night in your dream? That should have told you something. If you were halfway perceptive, you wouldn't have come out on the highway today." Death shrugs.

"Yeah, come to think of it, I did see you there. You were smiling and beckoning to me. The mood in the dream was warm and cozy and I wanted to run to you, but something told me to stay away.

You know how we all feel about you, Death. You're real difficult to like. Too many things to give up to be with you: cigarettes, Jack Daniels, sex, novels, music, dancing, movies, dope, coffee, sugar. I can't see it personally. Give it all up for what, Death? What do you have to offer?"

"Lean a little further to the right of the road and I'll show you."

Jane slows down and lets a large truck pass by.

"Uh-uh. Not on your life, Death. I'm not moving in front of that truck. That's not the way I want to meet my maker. I might, I just might, consider going over the bridge when we get to Joliet, but I am not going to get it on the tollway with these trucks."

"Not very daring, are you?" Death asks.

"No. I told you I don't even want you around. Why are you here? Why me?"

"I'm here because you came courting me. I want to be with you. You can't keep your car in the right lane. You keep weaving and shaking so bad, you can't drive and you think you don't want me? Ha."

"Could you get me a Valium?" Jane asks. "I've got one in my purse. Could you get it for me? Just a half. I can't take a whole five milligrams."

"Afraid to fall asleep on the highway or what?" Death smiles sweetly.

"Fuck you, Death. Fuck you."

Death laughs.

"That won't get you out of this one," he says.

"What can I give you to get out of my car? I can't play chess, so that's out of the question, and I don't have any cards with me. All I have with me is enough money to pay for the tolls. Maybe some for lunch. How would you like a nice lunch at Coffeeplace? Of course, it's not the same as me fixing you a special meal, but if you're hungry, I'll treat you. Is it a deal: I-55 instead of 297? Can you dig it, Death? Can you?"

"I don't know. I'm not supposed to lunch with clients. I'll have to think about it." Death is pensive.

Jane's car settles down and stays in her own lane a little better. She feels a huge surge of relief ... until she notices a bridge looming ahead.

Jane begins to panic again.

Better a bridge than a truck, she thinks.

Death just smiles.

"Death, can I ask you a question? I really am curious. I can't tell what sex you are. Are you a man or a woman?"

"That's real cute," says Death. He is silent.

Jane can't think of anything else to say so she concentrates very hard on keeping her car on the road, which isn't easy because it keeps sliding to the right of the shoulder or straddling the line in the middle. Jane is a wreck and Death knows it.

By the time they reach the Coffeeplace, Death is exhilarated.

"Beautiful drive, beautiful drive ... so relaxing." He gets out of the car and stretches.

Jane hates him. She has decided he is a *he* because a *she* wouldn't do this to her — sisterhood being powerful and popular and all that. This would be a definite no-no.

Jane climbs out of the car. She is shaking so hard, she has to lean against the car to steady herself. I'm going to take a Valium as soon as I get some water, she promises herself.

Death stands holding her prescription bottle in his hand, jiggling it up and down. He sticks it in his pocket. He is laughing.

"Come on. Let's go order our last lunch. Shall we get it to go?" He is doubled over, hysterical.

Jane wants to beat the shit out of the son of a bitch. He looks, of course, as if he might be a tad stronger than she is.

They go into the restaurant and sit down. Jane's face is ashen; Death is rosy and smiling. Jane drains the water from the glass at the table. She glances at the menu.

"Look, Death," she says. "Don't get any big ideas on what you're going to eat. Because the fact of the matter is, I don't have much money." She counts her money. "All I've got is $4, so don't look at the sirloins on the menu. Matter of fact, I was just thinking we might split something, looking at these prices."

"That's okay. Food's not too important to me. You order for us. I'm not used to eating out."

The waitress stands ready with her pad. Jane looks up.

"We'll have a bowl of vegetable soup. Is it homemade?"

"Yes, Ma'am," the waitress answers.

"And a grilled cheese and some french fries. And I'll have a Coke to drink."

She looks at Death. "What about you? Want anything to drink?"

"Water's fine." Death smiles. He is so amiable.

"I'm pretty disgusted with you, Death, to tell you the truth. I just wanted a nice drive today and you've made that impossible."

Jane takes a book out of her purse and begins reading, ignoring Death as he sits there looking smug and self-satisfied.

The waitress brings the order. Jane tastes the veggie soup.

"Not too bad," she says.

"Too watery," Death says.

"Here, have half of this grilled cheese." Jane hands Death half of the sandwich. Death chomps into it and chews slowly.

"Velveeta," he says. "I hate Velveeta." Death looks ugly and dissatisfied. "These french fries aren't crisp, and they are cold and not done in the middle. I hate fat fries. Soup's watery and cold."

"There's no pleasing you, is there Death?"

"There are some things that please me. Obviously you haven't gotten to them yet. This lunch is not one of them. I can get better food than this at home."

"So can I," Jane agrees. "Maybe I should fix dinner for you at my place. You could plan the menu. I'm a good cook, Death, really, and I don't even have Velveeta at my house. I have good cheese, from the co-op. Lots of protein. You'd like it. What do you say?"

"No. I say no. I should have taken you on the bridge. No more deals." Death is adamant.

"That's what I don't like about you. You're so inflexible, so rigid, so final. No room for bargaining. No room for spontaneity. Yuck."

They finish lunch and Jane leaves a big tip. They leave.

"Remember, Jane. You made a deal: I-55 for 297."

"Yeah, I know, I know. But I don't feel ready yet, Death. You can't go before you're ready. My mother always told me about my number being called. It's not right yet, Death. I'm pretty tuned into myself. I think I'll know when it's time."

"In this business, Jane, I call the numbers. Yours is up next."

Death doesn't want to talk about it anymore.

Jane does. "Death, really, be serious. Tell me why it has to be me."

"Because where I work, you can't go back alone. I must take someone with me and last night you conjured me up in your dreams, so I thought you were interested. Now you want to play, stalling for time, making deals, trying new tricks."

"Okay, I understand. Just because I flirted with you didn't mean I was courting you. Get that straight first. Secondly, if you have to take someone back with you, I have relatives. You'd like my mother. She's afraid of everything. Just knock on her door and you'd scare her to death, ha-ha."

Jane laughs. Death doesn't.

"Offering me your mother. What a child — selfish, selfish. Ah, the joys of parenthood." Death is clearly disgusted.

"It's not so bad, Death. She's older than I am. She's had a miserable life. She's got emphysema anyway. I'm not cruel and callous. I'm realistic. What do you say? Is it a deal?"

"No," says Death. "I've chosen you. You've chosen me. We're going back together."

"I haven't chosen you, Death. I flirted with you, but now I'm trying to reject you. I am not interested in you. But I am willing to bargain."

Death leans forward in the car and begins playing with the knobs on the radio until he gets some music. "Stayin' Alive" by the Bee Gees blares loud over the box.

"Did you see that movie, Jane?" Death asks.

"Yeah. You?"

"Yeah. The bridge scene was my favorite."

Death opens the ashtray and removes the papers, candy wrappers and Popsicle stick. He sticks the garbage on the seat and lights up a Marlboro.

"Had to clean out the ashtray to use it," he says, as he flicks his ashes off. "You don't mind, do you?"

"Naw. I don't. By the way, can I have a cigarette? I gave up smoking two months ago, but this is definitely a high-stress situation."

"I know what you mean." Death taps a cigarette out of his pack and lights it for Jane.

"Thanks," she says.

"How do you want to go, Jane?" Death asks. "Off a cliff, into the ocean, rushing, rushing, the exciting rush when you reach the jagged rocks."

"No, no, no, no," Jane protests.

"Vampires? Werewolves? You believe in them?"

"No. German shepherds are the closest I get to that. They scare me."

"Yeah, that is a yicky way to go, definitely. German shepherds. Yuck." Death shivers. "Are you into roller coasters? I like the old kind, the wooden ones, the sounds."

"No. I told you Death, I'm not into adventure. I'm into pleasure. Which is why I'd like to let you out of my car, any time you're ready."

"Pleasure. Hmmm." Death is thinking about that.

"Sex, Death. That's how I'd like to go. Maybe in the bathtub with my vibrator plugged in. The ultimate orgasm," Jane says.

"God, what an idea. That's one I hadn't thought of. Perhaps I could bargain with you. I'd like to know how that would work out."

"Oh, grant me an extension, Death. Yielding to the struggle of life. The kinship with my machine. Oh please, Death, only 60 more miles. I'll give you a new perspective. Next time you meet a woman who wants to flirt with you, you'll have some new ideas, suggestions."

"I'll think about it. It would be more interesting than another highway accident. I get bored with these. I like something more titillating. A cliff fall, getting gored by a bull. Roller coasters are my favorite. Shootings are okay. I love strangulations. Choking is boring. Old age is too natural. Fire is fun. I like to get people when they're not totally ready. That's the most fun."

"You're a real asshole, Death. You know that?"

Jane smiles.

Sixty more miles.

The Ultimate Orgasm.

"Tell me, Death. Is there anything afterward?"

The Laundromat

I am at the Laundromat. How many hours, how many days, how many years have I spent here?

It is hot in here. In the winter, I go to the doughnut shop and get coffee and doughnuts. I fight with the kids in public, telling them they cannot have the round doughnuts with the chocolate icing and the big glob of cream in the middle. A laundromat for all seasons.

This laundromat is an awful place. I've only been in one "mat" that I liked. That was in Chicago on Rush Street. I was 18; my big sister, living on the "Gold Coast," was in her 20s. The laundromat was in between the bars. People brought their laundry in cloth bags and played chess while it was washing. I was easily impressed. There was a fireplace.

This one, though, is stark and ugly. Big balls of lint roll on the floor. Weirdos inhabit this place. Like the one I'm looking at now. He's short and skinny, kind of wiry skinny, and his hair is greased down. He is clicking his false teeth in and out. He shoves his upper denture out and in, out and in, to the rhythm of the washer. Does he know he is doing this? I cannot tell. Perhaps he does this all the time. Perhaps it is a habit, imbedded in his daily routine. Maybe he does it at the grocery store while walking down the aisles; perhaps it's necessary to select an appropriate rutabaga while clicking one's teeth. Who knows?

The washer whirls, shakes and shimmies like an African dancer. I readjust the clothes so it can finish its cycle, readying the inside of this dark wet hole so it reaches its climax. I close the lid. It goes again.

The man with the false teeth now has his ear on the top of his washer. He is listening to the activity within the cavity. I watch and wonder why anybody gets off on the sound of a machine. But then, what business is it of mine? I think about the machines I like to listen to. The hum of the fan. When I was very young and small, the sound of my mother's old Maytag washer.

I always watched my mother and grandmother do laundry. Grandma had very large bosoms and they hung down to her waist. She did not wear a bra, and hadn't for some years. She was not liberated; or maybe she was, in a sense. But I always watched to make sure she didn't get her tit caught in the wringer. That was the joke in the neighborhood at the time. The old lady who got her tit caught in the wringer. I used to think about it a lot. I thought about the pain, mostly. Once I read about a girl on a farm who got her long blonde ponytail caught in some kind of machine that does something with corn. Pulled her features right off her face, it said. I thought about that a lot.

I've decided the greasy clicker isn't really into the sound of the washer. I've decided he's neurotic and "mats" are places that he just can't stand to be in for any length of time. Therefore, he's listening hopefully for the spin cycle. I've figured that out by thinking that anybody nervous enough to be flipping their teeth out in public wouldn't be laid back enough to get into hums. Or would they? The questions remain unanswered.

There are other weirdos here, in case you're interested. He is not the only one.

You should see Weirdo Number Two. Next to him, the teeth-flipper is a godsend. Number Two was pushed out of his top bunk bed at a very early age by his brother. He has never been the same since. To look at him, you wouldn't know he's as weird as he is. I mean, he looks sort of okay. Not too bad looking. If you look in his eyes — well, that's another story. Something is definitely wrong; he doesn't have both oars in the water. When I am loading my washers, he comes up to me from behind and whispers in my ear, "Can I kiss the inside of your thighs?"

Why do I keep coming to the laundromat? The doughnuts?

A truck stops outside. Two young women — two tired, old-looking young women — begin unloading boxes of dirty clothes. Dirty clothes in cardboard boxes bother me. My baskets are ripped, but they are plastic. The handles are torn. I can't believe all the laundry these two have. The stuff doesn't even look worth washing.

The red button is on. The dance is over. Silence.

I grab a laundry cart and attempt to drag it over to my machine. The wheels are all fucked up and it will not go in the direction in which I pull. I push with all my might and get so mad, it goes flying in the air for a short distance. I almost knock over a rug rat playing happily on the floor with the lint balls. The rug rat goes squalling to his mother. She looks up from her wash and gives me an abusing look. The old I-don't-know-how-you-could-hit-my-baby-with-a-cart look.

I look back, giving her the same hateful glare. Lady, I want to say, this is one of the few times in my life I have come to the "mat" alone, sans squallers, and I ain't about to listen to some kid screaming — at me. Put him in the dryer, I want to suggest. I don't say anything to the irate mother. I cuss and kick the cart instead. I practically carry the damn thing over to the dryer.

I'm pissed.

I choose the speed and temp and drop in my dime. Nothing happens. I put in another dime. What's wrong? I don't know. I have gotten into the rhythm of it now, dropping dimes in like there's no tomorrow. If one dime won't work, perhaps there'll be something magic in another one. Who knows?

Nothing.

I go up to the laundromat attendant. "I lost 40 cents in the dryer," I say through clenched teeth.

"Which one?"

"Huh?" I ask.

"Which dryer?" the deviant asks.

I walk back down the aisle to see the number on the dryer. "Number 9," I yell.

"Nine, 10 and 11 don't work," he says.

I bristle.

I can see, at the rate the dryers are working, that more dimes will be necessary for me to get the hell out of here, away from the teeth-flipper and the deviant.

I put a crumpled dollar bill in the change machine to get dimes. It comes back out. I put it in again. It comes back out. I rifle through my purse, looking for a less crinkled dollar bill. You have to get money right off the goddamn mint to get it in these fucking change machines. Who carries crisp new dollar bills around, unless it's Christmas and you're giving them to some relative for a gift? That's the only time I have new money.

The third dollar works. There's something to those old superstitions. Third time's the charm. I now have a fistful of dimes, prepared to fight the dryers for all I'm worth.

I grab my wet laundry and transfer it to machines 5, 6 and 7. I will watch the other suckers here try to dry their things in 9, 10 and 11. I have a sense of superiority. I know something they don't. What a piece of knowledge to have.

The teeth-flipper looks like he is about to get in his dryer. He is leaning far into it, feeling his undershorts to see if they are dry.

I have the clothes into their respective dryers. I put in the dime. The dryer starts to go around. Success. Just in time. A line is forming. I have a smug smile on my face because I have three dryers.

There is no unity in this laundromat. No spirit of camaraderie here. No ma'am, this is every person for him or herself. The women with the pickup truck full of threadbare clothes are putting them in the washers. It seems like they have been doing this for some time. Goody-Two-Shoes next to me has her dryer items timed. At the precise minute, she reaches in and hangs up everything she takes out. Anally fixated, you can tell. The rest of the poor slobs are waiting in line — for the dryers that don't work.

My dryer stops.

I rush over. People edge in closer to my cart. And me. I open the door and give a good feel. Wet. Not damp. Wet. Not only that, the dimes didn't last 10 minutes.

I'm pissed.

I readjust the setting — normal, instead of permanent press. I go up to the deviant at the counter who is now busy accepting people's cleaning. "Hey, those dryers don't dry 10 minutes," I say.

"They dry six. Six minutes for every dime."

I feel cheated. I begin dropping in more dimes, wondering how much longer I'll have to stay here.

The rug rat is eating the lint. The teeth-flipper is still trying to get in his dryer. The angry people are watching me, hoping I'll take my clothes home wet so they can have my ineffective dryer. I glare at them, hoping they'll be smart enough to keep their distance.

I watch the dryers go around and around, thinking back to the time when I was little and we used to ride around in the dryers when there wasn't anything else to do. I feel like telling the teeth-flipper, "Go ahead. Get in. It won't hurt you. In fact, it's fun. We used to do it for entertainment. Maybe that's your problem. You haven't ridden in a dryer." I almost give him a boost.

Ah, the old ride-in-the-dryer routine. I remember it as if it were only yesterday. It was a hot summer night when there wasn't much going on in the neighborhood. Every time it got like that, which wasn't often, my friend Sharon would suggest riding in the dryer. It was so long ago — about 22 years ago. We must have been 11 — 10 or 11.

She had a thing for dryers and I shared it with her. Not the thing, just the experience. I was actually afraid to get in them, because I thought I'd die or something. But she loved it. She'd laugh so hard while she was in it and make faces. All I thought about when it was my turn was, I hope she doesn't walk out of here trying to be funny. They were the kind of dryers that opened from the outside. So while you were riding in them, if the door guard left, you were stuck in the dryer.

I remember thinking about that a lot, but I don't think I ever told Sharon that's what I was worried about. I'd think every time that I wouldn't ride, but we'd put the dime in and she wanted to be sure she was fair with me; she knew she got a longer ride and she wouldn't have left me with no ride at all. After all, she thought it was fun. A perfectly acceptable activity to pursue when there wasn't anyone around to play ditch 'em. It was hot, though. I remember that. Almost too hot to breathe. I died several times in those dryers.

She'd do the same thing with the double Ferris wheel. I worked at the fair with her one summer. We worked in a food tent that sold ham, lamb, ram, spam, buffalo, bison and barbecue. "Walk in. Sit down. Have a lunch. Have a cold drink. Hey! We got chairs for the ladies, tables for the babies. If they're over 18, I'll hold 'em. Hot doggie looking for a home. Arf, arf." I used to stand out there and imitate them. It was a stitch.

But every lunch hour we'd fill up with coney dogs and lemonade shake-ups, and then Sharon would want to ride the double Ferris wheel. Every day, I hoped she'd find a ride she liked to go on herself, without me. Or someone else to go on them with. It never happened.

I had the same feeling when the carney closed us in the Ferris wheel seat that I had when the dryer door closed. My fate was out of my control. Anything could happen. I remember my stomach trapezing up to my throat as the big wheel went over the little wheel. It lasted forever. I always thought those guys that operated the rides knew when they had somebody on them who was scared to death. They let you ride extra then.

I never threw up once.

Every lunch hour was spent in Happy Hollow, where dreams came true. Especially if you were a ride freak, like Sharon was. I remember putting my foot down just once. There was this ride that went around real fast and the floor fell out. You were plastered against the wall, the force of gravity keeping you there. That's all. Fast. Speedy. Round and round. Sharon told me about it, her eyes shining like she'd found secret treasures or had seen the freaks in the fair booth.

No. I remember saying no. I wouldn't go on that ride with her. She'd have to find someone else to go. She begged me just to go with her up the stairs and wait while she bought a ticket. I didn't go on that one. She loved it, though. Went on it every day after we finished the double Ferris wheel stint.

My clothes are finally dry. I begin to fold them up. Whites. Towels. Darks. Three piles. The same three piles I have had for years.

I have been going to the "mat" every week for six years. The washers are 50 cents. The dryers cost me $1.40 today. I usually have five washers. If I was good at math, I'd figure up how much money I've spent in mats over the years.

Two Whole Nutmegs

"Twenty years ago the Beatles were singing 'I Wanna Hold Your Hand,' and Theron held Tana's hand and that was the beginning. Fraternity boy meets sorority girl. It started on a blind date. That was in 1963."

Everyone clapped; I wiped a tear from my eye, hoping no one noticed. I glanced around the room to see if anyone else was crying. I didn't want to be the only one, the lonely one, which I was already because I was the unattached one. Couples seemed to nestle together, counting the years until they too would be able to have a 20th anniversary celebration.

And me? I was thinking of the morning. I had returned my son from weekend visitation. My ex-husband stood in his country home, looking lonely also; his second wife had left him. I stared at the two children we had created together and felt very much separate and alone.

Mistakes, I told myself, have no place in a 20-year celebration.

Theron read poems to Tana, who stood looking serious and expectant. I listened, lightly closing my eyes and mind to the jostling couples crowding me in the foyer. Someone took pictures. Theron and Tana's children stood on either side of them. It was too sweet, the scene too real. A couple that deserved each other. Be glad it happens, I told myself. Love is possible. Love doesn't have to be over at 40.

The prospects look dim, the morbid voice groaned inside. Miracles do happen, I repeated silently.

Tana was the forest, Theron read from his book of poems. She was a refuge. Birds and trees and honey and love, and I listened, sipping iced tea and feeling even more set apart. The champagne drinkers flanked me and I wished I was not on medication; champagne would be a way to make it through the party.

When the ceremony ended, Theron and Tana's little girl played a piece on the piano. The guests applauded.

Vegetarian fare for the occasion, Midwest zucchini in every dish — zucchini lasagna, zucchini sticks rolled in Parmesan, zucchini and rice. My zucchini didn't make it this year; I moved from my house before I had harvested even the tomatoes. Zucchini went in too late, but I remembered the years when the harvest was full. Zucchini bread. Zucchini casserole, layered with mozzarella and Parmesan cheese. I filled my plate with one of everything and blessed potlucks. Tabbulah. Salad. Bulgur. Curry.

In the living room, I sat on the floor and ate at the coffee table with a roomful of others. A newly-married man talked to me about his dreams for the future. He heard I was in business for myself; he admired what I was doing. I dreaded telling him that I had no health insurance, no life insurance and no weekly paychecks. An inner voice warned me to beware of the dark side — my tendency to brood, to close the venetian blinds in my mind, warding off light.

The marrieds, Chris and Christine, were giving out a recipe. "Lots of sesame seeds," she was saying. "Chris has friends on the East Coast. They own a restaurant and are publishing a cookbook. James Beard has eaten there several times. He has allowed them to quote him — several sentences."

I thought of my unpublished book and resented them knowing people who published. I never thought I'd sink that low — begrudging a cookbook being published. Who reads them all, I wondered. Do people read more cookbooks than fiction?

"Sesame seeds are the trick," Christine continued. "That's why Chris was so successful in this particular dish. We used lots of sesame seeds." I wondered if she ever wondered where the money to purchase sesame seeds was coming from. Did she, upon waking, look through cookbooks every day?

Chris put out his cigarette — the only smoker in the room, I noticed. He lectured on why one shouldn't put tahini paste in the blender.

I worried about money. Occasionally I nodded to the man on the floor next to me who was interested in my opinion. Should he go into business for himself? I told him truthfully that I didn't think becoming one's own social service agency would be profitable. He wanted to help people, he said.

I searched the room for someone with whom I could establish a reference point. I found him in the back of the room. He was tall and black. I went to school with his brother. He was attending the party with a woman who taught at the university. I knew her, and she had told me about her new lover. Somehow, my vision hadn't matched this man. She had recently divorced husband number two; I had expected her new man might be like the recent ex. He had been a conservative business professor. This man didn't look like business.

In the kitchen, a banana cream pie was falling apart. The heat, the rampant humidity, the champagne were getting to the guests. I was sober; iced tea had produced no highs. I maneuvered a piece of pie onto a paper plate. It oozed and I ate. Tasty.

A group of women were sitting in a circle in the dining room. I joined them, breaking their circle. The discussion was about vacation and cars that broke down along the way. Breakdowns. Something I could relate to. They poured transmission fluid in the wrong place. The part cost $280. "I can't believe you are telling that story in public," the lover told her storytelling mate.

I focused on a woman in the group whom I disliked. I had good reason, I reasoned. She was a counselor who had done me irreparable harm once. I had since bad-mouthed her to my friends, whom I now realized were her friends. I hoped she hadn't heard my words, although it didn't matter. I saw her as a bad therapist. She saw me as a hostile client. I didn't think a reconciliation was in order for either of us.

My afternoon sunburn was the topic of discussion when anyone came near me. "Where have you been?" university professors asked me. I didn't say what came to mind — that unemployment had been denied, I was caught on a technicality, broke, living without income, insurance, love and my children. I said, "The beach." Not the Springfield beach. Which beach? I assured them it was the Springfield beach, the grody place where the water smelled like a sewage treatment plant — slime everywhere. I sat in a lawn chair and plugged Hank Williams Jr. in my Toshiba and listened to him sing the pain out of my chest.

They had spent summers in Carmel, Monterey and Long Island. The counselor I didn't like said she just had to be near the ocean. I was glad I wasn't. One more temptation. Even more tempting were two whole nutmegs at home in the kitchen pantry. Two nutmegs will produce death, read the label at the food co-op. Two whole nutmegs? The thought surfaced often. Shredded? In a quiche? Eaten whole? Had anyone ever successfully died an organic death? Did Sylvia Plath know about the nutmegs?

From the ocean to the nutmegs. I pulled myself together, thinking that I was asked to share in a celebration. My sadness could be left outside the door, could be picked up on the way home. Be happy. Don't be so self-indulgent. I made the wrong choices; this was the price. It was the Jew in me, I thought, that was also crying, "The price is too high." Had I chosen right and behaved myself, I too would have had a husband to link arms with, a paycheck to share, to use to buy sesame seeds, a new cookbook. And a 20th wedding anniversary.

But the men I had chosen? Would they have lasted 20 years? The musician who fretted through my life, who took over with his instrument, who played his notes on my time? The computer professor who turned cold as his machines when I used an improper word or gesture? The dancer who shared my space and a line of other women stretching from Springfield to East St. Louis? The ex-husband, the rebellious one who had no one to rebel against?

At home, two teens sat on the couch talking about Ralph Lauren makeup — a subject I could not pretend to enjoy. I walked around the apartment looking for something to do, but ignoring it when I found it.

A folder sat on the table. Poetry workshop. A new gig I would try. It was scheduled to begin in two weeks. I prayed for warm bodies with hot checks. I read the folder. Ellen Bass, the instructor, wrote letters to her students. She lived with a man, but had two loves — teaching and writing. Maybe they would be enough.

Rage

I named her Rage and I'll admit it was a mistake. But it was the '60s then, and a lot of people were searching for something unique and unusual in names, searching for something politically reflective, working out ideas and ideals on the unborn. I named her what I felt at the time. What the heck — others did too. Some of the kids in her day-care co-op had names like Free, Storm, Chastity, Windy. Some of the big-star hot shots named their kids Sun and Moon and River.

I was feeling rage. Every morning when I awoke, I would lie in bed mentally conjugating verbs — I rage, I raged, I had raged, I am raging, I was raging, I had been raging, I will be raging.

I became rage. I wore red maternity clothes, sucked on raw meat. I was passionate about rage. I cultivated it like a gardener growing beets.

She grew and grew and, while other babies sucked milk, she was born with two teeth and she sucked blood. My nipples bled. Her first word was no. She liked to eat red things, especially cherry Popsicles, raspberry Jell-O, maraschino cherries. I was always happy when Thanksgiving came; she ate cranberries, raw and cooked. I grew beets, red cabbage.

As a baby, she raged. Screamed, cried, kicked, fussed. "Rage, settle down," I would cry, but she would not. It took me a long time to find something that would settle her, something that would soothe her. Luck was on my side. She liked the sound of trains and we had tracks in our back yard. She was comforted listening to the sounds. Eventually, I bought a record of train sounds. I silently thanked the creative person who made that record. What a mind, I thought. What a creative thing to do. How did he know I would need it?

In the end, I bought several records. I was glad, for once, that I was poor, that I lived on the wrong side of the tracks. I thought about the rich, surrounded by city parks with trees, trees, trees, and no trains, no tracks. I stayed in that house for years. When I finally got financially secure enough to buy a house, I gave the realtor explicit instructions: close to the tracks and good water pressure. The water pressure was for me; I liked long, hot showers. The tracks were for Rage. Why the sound of trains comforted her, I'll never know, but it was one of those things I did not probe.

I did worry about internalized rage, though. I blamed myself, felt guilty for all the rage I felt during my pregnancy. Why wasn't I happy? I could have named her Joy. She could have cooed, worn pinafores, carried a Raggedy Ann doll. Maybe rage was transmitted, like heroin, to the baby.

I was angry the night she was conceived. I'll never forget it. He talked me into it. I was young. He told me stories — stories about his inability to procreate, stories about an injury that would not allow him to father a child. I didn't know much about anatomy. I believed it. When I turned up pregnant, he turned away. He left town. I heard he married a woman from Maine. Once I drove out to see him, to show him, to make him atone for his sins. But it didn't work. He had moved away.

At the time I slept with him, I was angry about other things — that is, before I found him out, before I got pregnant, before he took off. He was one of those men who joined the civil rights movement, one of those men who registered voters in the south. I was angry working with them most of the time. I thought they were hypocrites, fanatics, middle-class suburbanites, armchair radicals. I thought I was the real thing: I knew poverty, I knew gangs, I knew them first hand. I knew struggle, knew it wasn't joyous. I didn't delude myself. I knew what I knew and it was better than anything from Political Science 101. I knew that. Rage. I felt rage.

Not that she didn't make out okay. To tell the truth, she did pretty well. She had an edge on everyone else. She was always angry, so adrenaline pumped through her veins like money into a rich man's bank account. Rage was ever present — it was moving, it was flowing, it was standard fare for her. Rage was more than a name. It was sustenance; it was force; it was energy. Rage. Pulling every direction, she could get mad about anything and she did — which worked in her favor, because she was little and pretty and had red curly hair.

Then she entered the public school system. There, one acquiesces; one does not rage. I tried to see both points of view. On the one hand, she had something to rage about. On the other hand, a teacher with 30 students full of rage could not teach much. One had trouble focusing on moods and tense of verbs when one was filled with rage.

I don't think she was ever happy. While I hoped maybe it was a stage she would grow out of, it wasn't. She didn't. It was a commitment, a way of life.

Of course, I felt guilty. Who wouldn't? I had friends who had kids who did what they were told and seemed quite pleased to please others. I remember a dance recital. Rage was supposed to be on stage, but she was not. She had locked herself in a closet and spent the whole night kicking and kicking and kicking a locked door. She was 3.

I thought about changing her name from Rage to Prudence, Mary, Angela, something calm, something that would change her disposition, but it didn't work. She raged when I mentioned a name change. For a while she said she wanted it, but as the time got nearer to make it official, she would refuse. I begged. Alison. Annamarie. Sherry. No, no, no. She would pull her red curls, stamp her feet, jump up and down, throw objects. She liked to hear the sound of plates hitting the wall. She liked china, glass dishes. I shopped at the Salvation Army and garage sales to keep cheap dishes around. Not that I had to make a special effort to own inexpensive things.

I took her to a therapist. The therapist blamed me for her name. I didn't know, I said. I didn't know names were important. I didn't know you became your name. I pleaded ignorance. Change her name, the therapist said. Shame on you.

I left feeling suicidal. I felt worse than I normally felt. I had paid $60 for 50 minutes to hear what I already knew. Only now it was worse, because prior to seeing the shrink, it had only been my opinion. Now it was the opinion of a qualified professional. In order to feel better about this miserable diagnosis, I remembered the words of my uncle: "You see those shrinks, girl, and that's exactly what they'll do — shrink your head." I had seen shrunken heads in shell shops in Florida, in voodoo. I pictured my head that way — shrunken, hanging, for sale.

I tried ignoring Rage's rage. I bought her punching bags, pillows, more train records. Everything seemed to help a little until she entered her teens. She dyed her hair various shades of pink, red, purple. She shaved bits and bits and bits of her hair until almost her entire head was shaved. She wore safety pins in her ears, cut off the cuffs and collars of her clothes, listened to rock groups that I thought were dangerous. But she stopped breaking plates. She lost weight continually, ate red foods, wore a red cape.

She was smart. While she did not excel in the traditional sense, she did get by in school — good grades, no output.

She saved her money — money she made from cutting hair, money from presents, money from working summers. After high school graduation, she left for California, took the Amtrak. Said she lives near the beach, works when she has to, still likes the sound of trains, but the roar of the ocean is alluring. She says she will save her money, go to UCLA, study biology. Says she calls herself Reggie out there. Says she thinks she might be done with a lot of her rage. Says in California, no one rages a lot. Says it's different out there. People are kicked back. She'll never live in the Midwest again. She needs sun and water, she says.

I watch women around me having babies in the '80s. Nobody seems particularly interested in naming kids Star and Moon, Sun and Wind, Earth and Fire. People are using family names, names of aunts and uncles — Aaron, Gretchen, Mary.

I miss Rage. I walk into her mostly red and purple room, stare at her bulletin board, look through her closet at the clothes that used to anger me so — those shirts with their cuffs and collars cut off, pins and clips and belts with studs. She sends me pictures sometimes, pictures of her standing by the ocean, wind in her red moussed curled hair. She does not look happy, necessarily. She does not smile. But she looks calm.

Out of habit, I go to garage sales and buy plates. I stockpile. I want to throw them. I want to show them.

Peace in the Valley

"Peace in the valley," Elvis croons on TV. His biggest fan, my mother Ella, stands with legs apart, wedgies — oh those shoes! — and she sways while he sings. She stares at the long ash on her cigarette, breathing every emphysema breath. A Marlboro, sucking it in.

"Look at him, Angel. Ain't he handsome?"

Ella coos and swoons. She has been in love with the King since 1957 when she quit her job, withdrew her money from the State Employees Retirement Plan and went to Memphis to live out her fantasy. Ella and Elvis, together forever. Eventually, Uncle Phil found her working at a car wash. Heartbreak Hotel.

"Honey, don't you think he's handsome? Listen to him sing. I wish you could find someone like Elvis to marry. He's a nice religious boy." She stares at the TV and back to her ash.

"You want me to find someone like that?" I say. I want to call him a dope fiend or pervert, but that would alienate Ella.

"He's a good actor. This is a real good movie."

"You can't be serious," I say, looking up from my novel. I am reading *The Awakening* by Kate Chopin. After *Moby Dick*, it is a find. I am on the wicker chaise lounge. Ella is in front of the TV. "Actor? Orson Welles is an actor. Bogart. Clark Gable. Elvis is hardly an actor."

"I think he's good."

Elvis is a rock-and-roll cowboy singing about being lonesome and travelling all alone — "If you don't call me, baby, then I'm never coming home." A greasy curl hangs over his forehead. He is young, thin, has an innocent look. Legs spread apart, he plays his guitar. Ella swoons.

"God, look how baggy his pants are," my daughter Anastasia says. She has come in from playing kickball.

"Shhh," Ella says. "He's the King."

Elvis sings, "I've got a woman mean as she can be. Sometimes I think she's almost as mean as me."

In the movie, the girls scream and swoon. In the living room, Ella sways and trances, trances and sways. Finally, a commercial.

"Ain't he wonderful? Look how handsome he is. And he can move. He's so sexy."

"Yeah," I say, quoting a line from the movie. "Looks like he's got jumping beans in those jeans."

Elvis is Deke Rivers. He stands in a hotel room with his agent, an older, sophisticated, attractive blonde. "You are about the only one who ever had faith in me, Miss Linda," he says.

Ella wipes tears from her eyes. "Ain't that sad, Angel? I've got faith in him. I always have."

"Is Grandma crying?" Anastasia asks. "Over Elvis?"

"Grandma loves Elvis," I say. "You know that."

"But why? He's so ugly."

"Shush," Ella says. "I want to hear this part."

Elvis and his agent Linda are in the cemetery. Elvis confesses. His real name isn't Deke Rivers. He took the name off a tombstone. "I don't know any more about him than I do about me," Elvis says. "He didn't have anybody either."

The floodgates are unleashed.

I hand Anastasia a box of tissues to give to Grandma, who is bawling in front of the TV.

"Gosh, Grandma must really like Elvis. I've never seen her cry."

"She gets emotional about him," I say.

Elvis is with his true love Susan, the country singer whose talents are no longer needed in the band since he came along. But Susan doesn't care. She's in love with Deke. He won her a bird at the fair. He sings "Loving You."

It's too hard to keep my mouth shut. "Look, Ella. These Presley movies are so amateur Freudian. He talks about his mother. How he was abandoned. An older, sophisticated woman is blonde and evil. A young farm girl is pure. He's drawn to evil, but good triumphs. He never has sex. One kiss. Elvis, the innocent victim."

"You can be so nasty, Angel. How can you say such things? That blonde woman was bad. And good does triumph over evil, if you believe it does."

"If you say so."

"I'm glad you let me stay over to watch this movie. I'm sure glad he ended up with Susan and not that other one." She packs her cigarettes in her taupe leather bag. "Give Grandma a kiss," she says to Anastasia. She leans her cheek down to Anastasia, who has flipped the channel and is watching Dick Van Dyke. "I wish I could see him in Las Vegas. That would be a dream come true."

"I think you'd be disappointed. I don't think he looks like he did tonight on TV. That movie was made in 1957, over 20 years ago."

"Oh, he's still handsome, honey. He's still the King."

I think of Elvis before he died. Bloated from drugs. Watching people have sex. The Perverted King. I go back to my book. When she leaves, I don't look up.

Kitty

He was lying on the bed in the dining room when I came home from work.

"He's going to die," Anastasia said. "Bridget said that's how her cat looked before he died."

"Is he going to die?" I asked.

I kept asking everyone in the house. Is he going to die? The same question.

Lyn came home from work. She went immediately to the dining room and lay on the bed with George. I didn't know she was there. I was busy stirring the soup.

Anastasia came in and watched as the soup swirled.

"Lyn is still in there talking to George," she said.

"Is she?" I asked. That's all I could say these days. Is he? Is she?

I looked at Lyn, stroking his fur. Tears were dripping down her sweet face.

"Does he have it?" I asked Lyn, with the same detached monotone that I had been using to ask all of my questions these days.

"He's so sick," she said. "He's gotten so much worse."

She went upstairs.

I continued to prepare food until I realized I had on my panty hose from work. They didn't have cotton liners so I remembered that I should change them.

As I went into my bedroom, I could see Lyn talking on the phone in the hallway. She took the phone into her bedroom when she heard me. She was talking to her mom. Long-distance. I heard her crying.

"I like to imagine him playing with Kitty," she said. "In heaven. Or imagine that he will be anywhere I want him to be."

We've lived together eight months, I thought. Can't she cry in front of me? Is that another difference between the rich and poor? The old rich never cry in front of anyone. The poor are too tired to care. No one has ever told them not to talk about money in public, or not to cry in front of people.

I knew how she felt. I was out of tears for George, if you want to know the truth. I wasted them all on Kitty. I still cry over Kitty. A cat-hater crying over a Kitty, one month after the fact. A cat-hater dreaming about Kitty. And Kitty's mother — Momcat, we called her. And George. He was there too, in the dream. They were all crawling around the screened-in porch that used to be outside my bedroom in the house I lived in some 10 years ago. Yes. The three of them were there.

Panty hose off, I went downstairs to continue to prepare dinner. We were having steak tonight — one steak, that is. I was fixing it for Anastasia, who said she didn't feel like eating. I was really fixing it for Lucy, the dog. Lucy hadn't had any meat for a long time. In a vegetarian kitchen, a good dog could suffer. Lucy had been suffering.

Lucy was the replacement for Kitty. So far it hadn't worked. The dog was supposed to be Anastasia's pet. With a dog, surely she could forget Kitty.

George was dying, and while I prepared supper, I had to get into the cabinet to get something. Gerber baby food — chicken — stared out at me while I grabbed the garlic.

Kitty. Anastasia fed her baby food the last week. I poked pills down her throat, trying to prolong her days. We didn't know how long it would be. How long does it take a cat to die?

It's funny. I remember Lyn was the first to notice something was wrong with Kitty. "I think she's sick," she said. "Look how matted her fur looks. Kitty's fur never looked like that."

I hadn't noticed.

"She's been acting funny," Lyn said. "She hasn't been herself lately."

She hadn't. I didn't notice.

"I think she needs to see the vet," Lyn said. "Her ribs are poking through. Here. Feel."

I had to feel Kitty's ribs. Yes. Lyn was right. They were poking through. How did she notice these things?

"I'll take her to the vet," I said. At first, I think I really complained about the money. But the more I thought about it, the more I thought I owed it to Kitty.

Anastasia and I took Kitty to the vet. He took one look at her and said she might have leukemia. Leukemia? Do cats get leukemia? Can it be cured? It's highly contagious among cats? How about humans? Will we die too? Are you sure you're not mistaken? Could it be something else? Something less final?

We waited for the test. Anastasia began feeding her baby chicken food. I gave her pills. She stayed on Anastasia's bed for a week. Anastasia stayed home from school for a week. I let her do it; she told me she had a sore throat. I believed her. She and Kitty watched soap operas. Kitty didn't watch; she slept. Anastasia watched soaps and cut out paper doll clothes while Kitty slept at her feet.

"You should put her to sleep," friends suggested. "Pay the fee and have her put to sleep."

I know I'm funny about paying vets money. Any doctor, for that matter. But it didn't feel right. I couldn't picture Kitty in a cold, white, sterile clinic with some doctor who didn't know her putting a needle in her arm. Her paw. Wherever they put it. I couldn't see the picture in my mind. When I can't picture things in my mind, I can't do them. It's that simple.

"She's going to die at home," I told Anastasia.

She agreed.

Well-meaning friends didn't understand. Why put Kitty through all that misery? Well, for one thing, she didn't seem miserable. She just slept. The night before she died, she looked in Lyn's eyes and gave a loud meow that sounded like a question. Sorry, Kitty. We didn't do a very good job of giving an answer.

We really had no idea how long it takes a cat to die. It didn't take very long. About a week, I guess.

George was the first to know. I came home alone one night. Everyone was gone for the night. Lyn was out of town. Anastasia was at her father's house. I was alone in this big scary house. George was with me.

Kitty was down in the basement. George wanted out of the house. It was 2 a.m. "No," I told him. "You have to stay with me. I'm frightened." George stayed because he was a gentleman.

I remember when he first came in the house. Lyn said he must have lived in a home sometime. "He washes himself when he's in the house," Lyn said. "I've never seen him do that outside."

I used to wonder how she knew so much about cats. When the hell time did she have to see who was washing themselves where. I'd missed it all.

George was an alley cat who came to us when he saw Kitty. When she was 5 months old, white, furry and beautiful, we let her out on the porch for the first time. He came along and started to carry her off the porch. We caught him.

I used to think of him as a rapist then. Raping a 5-month-old kitten. Really. I was annoyed. I thought she was too good for him. He was just a gray short-haired alley cat. She was a Persian-type longhair with a magnificent personality.

After Lyn mentioned it though, about him washing himself, I began to notice George. Lyn loved him. Against our will, she brought him into the house.

I was determined not to love him. I resented him every time he ate out of Kitty's bowl. She would walk around her dish and sniff. Then she wouldn't eat. I figured she wasn't happy with George sharing her litter box and food. I didn't like it either.

Anastasia and I would gossip about how we didn't really like George. He really wasn't our sort. We resented his intrusion on her private space. We felt so protective of Kitty. Our Kitty. Found in the woodpile in California by Anastasia and one of her newly-found friends. I loved her mother, Momcat. Mom, we called her for short. She was so independent.

I really did love her. The first cat I ever even liked.

George howled the night Kitty died in the basement. He stood in the hallway at 2 a.m. and cried a mournful cry. I yelled at him. "What the hell's the matter with you, George? You're not going outside, George," I told him. "I'm scared. You're staying with me."

His cry sounded like a cross between a coyote howling and a Yiddish chant that my uncle did on my grandmother's grave the day of her burial. It was a cry of death.

I didn't know that then. It seems like I never knew what anything was about until it was over. I knew George was dying, though. He just went downstairs to the basement.

Anastasia stood by the basement door and said, "Oh-oh. He's going down to the basement. That's what Kitty did. He's going to die."

Lyn protested. "Don't talk like that," she said.

He was one of the neatest cats, besides Kitty. He was big and strong and at night when I was alone, I felt like he was protecting me. I imagined him the size of a lion, I suppose. He was so big and strong. He was very heavy. Kitty was light and fluffy. You could pick her up with one hand. It took two hands to pick up George.

Lyn said he really thought he was a stud. When he walked, his balls shook back and forth. They were rather large.

I think he and Kitty would have had children. I mean kittens. But Kitty aborted. I was at a training seminar in Chicago. When I got home, there was blood on the sofa. My lover, who had been staying with Kitty and Anastasia, said that Kitty had passed some kind of purplish fetus.

I had dreamed, in Chicago at the seminar, that everyone at the seminar had aborted a fetus; they were purple and red. It was so clear, the dream. Then Kitty did. The same time I dreamed it. Can a person be tuned into a cat?

I took her to the vet. He said her uterus was enlarged and she should have it out. I probably would have gone along with it, but the fee was $55. Too steep, I thought. Besides, one litter of kittens would be nice.

We had never had any kittens except when Momcat had Kitty and Silver Claws. Silver Claws was killed out in front of the house in California. Anastasia cried and cried.

She cried and cried in the vet's office too, when the vet said Kitty had leukemia. We tried and tried to get that vet to tell us she would live, but he wouldn't tell us.

Lyn was crying now because George was dying. Do cats bring death? Anastasia asked me why Kitty had to die. She was so good and pretty and everyone loved her. Why did she have to die?

Anastasia kept asking me that. I was not religious; I did not know the answer to that. So I asked my lover Fidel. He was very religious.

He sent a card with a kitty on it — a white kitty like Kitty. The kitty was sitting in a boat with an owl who was playing a guitar. The card had a purple-blue background with a moon and stars. There was a large jar of jam and gold coins in the boat.

This is what the card said: "What do you think of this card? Kitty is up in heaven. She took a boat there and ate jam and counted gold coins and listened to glorious love songs about us. The world's greatest lovers. Kitty is playing hide and seek in the white clouds and waiting to jump on an eagle's back for a ride. Kitty had to die because dying is part of living."

Leave it to somebody religious to explain death. Dying is part of living. I was a separatist. I didn't look at it at all like that. As far as I was concerned, dying was dying and living was living. People who can't make connections are stupid, I told my friends.

I was comforted by those words. I told them to myself when I cried over Kitty. Dying is part of living.

George went down and sat in an old box top tonight — you know, the lid of a box. Lyn went down to talk to him. He raised his eyes, looked her straight in the eye and meowed.

Then he got up and went to a dark, private spot behind the furnace.

Chapel of Love

Out of the corner of her eye, Mrs. Peterson noticed a young woman embroidering seed pearls on the bodice of a wedding gown. The young woman sat on the floor, cross-legged, and concentrated on each stitch. She wore a black derby, a white T-shirt and black tights. A young man stood next to her, watching the planes come in. He wore a Cubs T-shirt with the printed names and faces of four players: Ryne Sandberg, Mark Grace, Andre Dawson and Shawnon Dunston. His left arm was bandaged.

Mrs. Peterson knitted while she waited for the Funjet to Las Vegas. Occasionally, she looked up. Her eyes met the eyes of the young woman.

"That's a beautiful dress," Mrs. Peterson said. "Did you make it?"

"Yes," the young woman said. "I'm all finished except for these pearls." She held the bodice up so Mrs. Peterson could see. "I've got to finish by 6 o'clock tonight because we're getting married."

"Really?" Mrs. Peterson said. She put her knitting down. "In Las Vegas?"

The young woman nodded. The young man turned from the window and looked at Mrs. Peterson. After a long pause, he said, "You look familiar."

"I don't think I know you. But my name is Marie Peterson."

The young man snapped his fingers. "I knew it. I knew I knew you. You're Mike Peterson's mom, aren't you?"

He turned to the woman on the floor who was threading her needle.

"Trudy, that's Mike Peterson's mom." He pointed at Mrs. Peterson.

Trudy looked up briefly and smiled. Then she looked back down at her sewing.

"I'm Jim," the young man said. "And this is Trudy. We've been over to your house a couple of times. In fact, Trudy and I met because of Mike. We met through his bulletin board. The one he had on his computer."

"Oh, that," Mrs. Peterson said. "That was years ago. We lived in Winnetka then."

"Yeah. In that big green house. And Mike used to have a dog. What was his name? He was kind of a funny color." Jim scratched his head. He had a crew cut with a design etched into one side.

"Pinka," Mrs. Peterson volunteered, continuing to knit one, pearl two.

"Pinka," Jim repeated. "What happened to that old dog? Is he still alive?" Jim sat down on a chair across from Mrs. Peterson and next to where Trudy was sitting on the floor.

Mrs. Peterson looked up. "No," she said. "He died last year."

Trudy stopped sewing. She stared off into space for a moment. "Aw, that's too bad," she said. "I just hate it when your pet dies." A tear fell.

Mrs. Peterson reached into her purse for a tissue and handed it to Trudy. Afterward, she picked up her knitting and began to talk.

"Of course we were all sad. But don't cry. Pinka was very old for a dog. He was 16 when he died, you know, and in such awful pain. He had these terrible running sores. I had to pick him up every time he wanted to go to the bathroom and carry him outside. He was very heavy. It was probably a blessing that he died when he did."

Trudy put her sewing basket on the chair next to Jim. She held her wedding gown out like an offering. "Will you hold this?" she asked Mrs. Peterson. "I have to go to the bathroom before the plane takes off."

"Certainly," Mrs. Peterson said. She studied the label in the back of the gown and saw that it was not made by Trudy.

Jim played with the edges of his gauze bandage.

"Don't mind Trudy," he said, not looking up from his activity. "She's just upset, that's all."

"Upset? On her wedding day? The poor dear. I can't imagine why she is so upset about our old dog. She couldn't have met him more than twice. I would have remembered." Mrs. Peterson scrutinized Trudy's sewing of the seed pearls.

Jim held his arm out to the side and sat back in his chair. "It's just that Trudy lost her cat yesterday. Her cat was killed."

Mrs. Peterson frowned. "Oh, that is too bad. What happened? Did it get hit by a car? Or was it feline leukemia?" Mrs. Peterson's own cat had died of leukemia in 1981.

"No," Jim said. "It wasn't leukemia. My pet snake Elvis killed Trudy's cat. It was terrible." He pointed to his bandaged arm. "That's how I got this. I tried to stop Taffy — that was Trudy's cat — from sticking her paw under the door. Before I could get to her, Elvis got her."

"That is horrible," Mrs. Peterson said. She put Trudy's dress aside and took up her knitting again. "The poor girl. What kind of a snake was it? And how exactly did this happen?"

"Elvis was a boa constrictor," Jim said. "Actually he still is. Trudy never liked my snake. He was a present from this girl I used to go with, Sally. Elvis was pretty big. He weighed about 85 pounds. I kept him in the bathroom with the door closed. You know, I have kind of a computer business in my home and people come over and stuff." He rubbed the zigzag design on the side of his head. "Taffy hadn't been staying with us, but since we're getting married and all, Trudy brought her over from her grandmother's. Trudy was very attached to that cat." Jim's left leg began to shake.

"What happened then?" Mrs. Peterson asked. She was eager to hear the whole story so she could tell Mike and her sister, whom she was meeting in Las Vegas.

"Well," Jim said. "Elvis was in the bathroom with the door closed when Taffy ran up the stairs and stuck her paw under the bathroom door. Elvis must have grabbed her with such force that it threw her against the door and hit her head so hard it killed her. I saw it about to happen, so I ran upstairs, but I must have grabbed Taffy just as she was dying because she bit me."

He raised his bandaged arm. "It really hurts. I had to have my neighbor take me to St. Luke's emergency room. Good thing he was home. This all happened yesterday."

Jim shook his head. He frowned. "Then I had to get rid of Elvis. Trudy wouldn't come back into the house unless I got rid of him. I ended up driving to Wisconsin to a pet store that bought Elvis for $75. I hated to part with him. I've had him for four years. I loved him. You know how you are with your pets." He stared at Mrs. Peterson.

Mrs. Peterson pursed her lips and shook her head. "I don't see how anyone could love a snake," she said. "I mean, a snake is not like a dog or a cat. A dog becomes your friend and waits for you to come home and all. And a cat sits in your lap and purrs and is happy to see you. But a snake."

She shook her head again and began to knit. After a short pause, she looked back up at Jim and asked, "What did you feed him? And where did he go to the bathroom?"

"The feeding was a little complicated," Jim admitted. His story was interrupted by the announcement over the loudspeaker that the airplane was about to board. All passengers who required special assistance were asked to get in line and have their boarding passes ready.

Mrs. Peterson put her knitting into a bag and searched for her ticket. Trudy returned. Her mascara was smeared and her cheeks were red and splotchy. Mrs. Peterson held the gown out to her.

"I had a hot dog," Trudy said. "It was kind of rubbery and way too expensive, but it made me feel better." She smiled at Mrs. Peterson. "I hope I can get this finished," she said, examining the pearls on the bodice.

Mrs. Peterson got in line to board the plane. Trudy and Jim were behind her.

"Where are you getting married?" she asked Trudy.

"The Chapel of Love," Trudy said. "It's right on the Strip, next to the Wild West Hotel. Why don't you come? The wedding's at 6. We'd love to have you there. It will be fun. We're going to have it videotaped and you could show it to Mike. I bet he'd like that."

"I'll try to come," Mrs. Peterson said. "I'd love to see you in the lovely dress."

"Rabbits," Jim whispered to Mrs. Peterson, as she boarded the plane. "I fed Elvis rabbits. Bought them at the pet store. Feeding Elvis wasn't such a problem. Snakes don't eat like every day or anything. They're not like dogs, if you know what I mean."

Mrs. Peterson nodded and handed her boarding pass to the checkpoint person. She still wanted to know where and how snakes defecated and whether Trudy had lied about making her dress. She was eager to attend the wedding. It sounded more interesting than attending weddings of people she knew. Once she had attended a stranger's funeral. She had read in the local newspaper that a woman with her same name had died. She had gone to the funeral and found it much more appealing than other funerals she had attended. This Marie Peterson had hundreds of relatives and friends. It looked like she had led a charmed life.

Mrs. Peterson made a mental note to tell Mike about Trudy and Jim. Maybe she'd call him from Las Vegas. She hoped Trudy would get the pearls done on time.

Poems

Bad Blood

I.   She is your sister.
Her red cells are destroying white cells.

      A doctor calls from Chicago, tells you she is dying. "In an emergency measure, we removed her spleen."

      When you arrive, she tells you she is not dead yet.

      You stay all night in a hotel with your older sister: she gets crabs and you do not.

      Your sister lives, but doctors do not know why.

      "An allergic reaction to Nyquil," they say.

      Twenty-seven years later, you want your sister to buy life insurance. The company says, "Extensive blood work required." Your sister refuses.

II.   He is your son, your youngest child, born red but turns chalk-white, blue.

      You take him to six doctors in six weeks. A doctor orders a blood count and sends him to the hospital for a transfusion.

      "His hemoglobin dropped. We don't know why. We're lucky he's alive. One more week and he would have been dead."

      He is pink, but not whole. At 23, he can't read.

      You find out he has extra pieces on six pairs of chromosomes. You puzzle over the connections.

III.   She is your older sister. She has three cancers: spinal column, bone marrow and blood. Multiple myeloma: a rare form of blood cancer that occurs in blacks more than whites, men more than women. Your sister is white.

The Graduate Assistant's Lament

>> I am tired

> I am angry

I am tired of being angry

I am tired of policies, simple things made
difficult, institutions, the
inaccessibility of public places,
overextension, hypertension and loose ends.
I am tired of memos, rules, parking stickers,
too much snow, and not being able to afford
> car insurance.
> I shun
committees, executive and otherwise.

I am tired of the tightness in my neck,
the tightness in my throat, and stifled
creativity. I am tired of power and I am tired of not
having any. I am tired of dehumanizing
situations, computer print-outs, sterile
grocery stores, neon signs, fast food chains,
slenderalls with no lumps, commercials, dishes,
laundry, no seat covers in my car with
the stuffing coming out.

I am tired of planning brown bag lunch sessions
and I am tired of attending them. I am tired
of collecting copy, correcting copy and putting
copy together. I am tired of writing up minutes,
meetings, making policy and I would rather make
coffee. I am tired of subscriptions, decisions
and guilt. I am tired of rejection slips, Freudian
slips, past due slips and half slips that are too
tight around the waist. I am tired of one-night stands
and I am tired of ongoing relationships. I am tired of
friends and I am tired of lovers and
I am tired of the distinction. I am
tired of the Movement and I am tired of no movement. I
am tired of going to class and I am tired of everything,
everyone, everywhere. I am tired of dirty socks, hairy legs, greasy
hair and those two goldfish I have tried to kill but live on. I

am tired of frosted Mini-wheats, peanut butter, running out of rice, the telephone, not having any money for dope, dread and anxiety.

I am tired of too many people needing me and I am tired of needing too many people. I am tired of plants, poverty, pimples and the past and I am tired of the now and the future. I am tired of shabby exams and piss-poor papers that make no points. I am tired of sexism, racism, mites, red spiders, disorganization, confusion, chaos and confessions true or false, mine or others'. I am tired of ugly clothes, laundromats, gas stations, license plates and the Salvation Army. I am tired of fear and I am fearful of complacency. I am tired of form and I am tired of formlessness. I am tired of not getting mine and I am tired of getting too much. I am tired of my glass-top table with no glass and three boards that don't fit, sickly plants, soiled pillows, dishes, garbage, dirty dishtowels, schedules, plans and waiting for my main man to show up. I am tired of fighting the urge for a cigarette and I am tired of succumbing to it. I am tired of crisis, rape, abuse, violence, domestic or otherwise. I am tired of no single answers and too many questions tire me out.

so what?

you've turned me off
thoroughly from thoreau
don't bore me
i know what's on page 11
i am flunking
my oxalis has mites
fingers stick in the
typewriter keys
it's hot and
      i'm horny

Untitled

Brainchild is a blueberry bush.
Stories fall in clumps, like berries,
some luscious, some not quite ready,
waiting for sun and time to ripen them.

Like berries, stories need nurturance.
Brainchild is the irrigation, the water.
I relish these morsels, gobble them up,
the sweet and the bitter.

Time

Those early morning
hours wait patiently
like a mother.
Hands circle wide
like a dancer.
They seem not to cry,
but to whisper gently
oh use me — write.

The Pause in Between

She used to have a period but
now she has a point of exclamation!
She used to have a period but now
she is like a comma, pausing, pausing,
no complete stop she used to have
a period but now she has a swollen
semi-colon

she used to have a period but now
she feels like a dash — punctuated
and mechanically correct — an
informal mark.

Feminists Need Cents

She offers not
who haseth not
money, pie nor power
for before our sisters
open our cage
they must make more
than minimum wage.

Filing

I have a great filing system
in my house
letters from the Governor concerning
ERA are filed in my Shakespeare book;
no certain order, of course, just stuck.

Two three by five cards with notes
from speech and a dance class receipt
are stuffed in *No More Masks.*
Dreams are wadded up and pushed
into a raggy yellow envelope
Manuscripts to work on are labelled
as such and stuffed into a
a whole, like tuna in tomato.

No Piecemeal Deal

Your inner rage is unbecoming,
let it fade.
I won't obey the invisible lines
drawn around you.
I run right through the yield signs
posted in your psyche.

A Good Old Time

When I get a piece
        of pie
It's not usually
        economic
        maybe
cherry or ass or pecan

I'm having a very
        good time
waitressing three hours
        a day
child to raise, bills to pay

degrees, degrees
whyamistillonmyknees?

Meek and mild
my manner sickens me
makes me prey
for all the nothing
that comes along.

Untitled

But she thought
when she looked at the
clear light blue sky
about the dark blue
gray clouds flowing
on together as one mass
part tufts, here and there
the outline of black birds against the sky
songs of birds and crickets
she thought maybe this is it
maybe as she watched the sun come up
go down
listening maybe that way was
the best.

On the Verge Of

There is a woman
that comes to the fountain
to watch the colors.
Gray, green, silver, blue, quivering
        reflections in
the water.
She watches, lost in thought.
Her only child is gone. Will someone
share her grief?
The colors bounce, bow and sway
like dancers.

She does not participate.

Recipe

1 1/2 cups leftover schizophrenia
1/2 cup split personality soup with ham bits
1/4 cup minced words
1/8 cup dehydrated libido
2 tablespoons paranoia
1 pinch hysteria
1/2 cup belligerence
2 ounces catatonic stupors
1 cube hallucinations
a pinch of monosodium glutamate to retard spoilage

Serving suggestions:

Stew for a few years.
Can be stuffed away in little Tupperware containers
until company comes. If frozen, allow 24 years to
thaw.

Recipe from Rosie and Pippy

Untitled

My family thinks I'm mad
because I hate them
but actually I hate them
because they are mad

you called me sister
because you wanted me to
listen to your problems
but I didn't want to

Maybe I should have been
more direct and said so
but I thought I'd try it
one more time

it was the same game and
i'm sick of denial, I am
sick of blame and failure
and sickness and

I can't listen anymore
Don't call me up to talk
of anyone's problems I
am not available for

problems I have my own
to take out and pore over
I do not want yours
I will not accept me them you us

don't give me no long distance guilt
It's as bad as the down home kind
I am done, dear family,
playing your game.

Marking Time

Mother waited five years
        underground
for a monument to validate
        her departure

The daughter has chosen well
gray granite with mother's three names
Star of David and a primrose
the February flower

Thirty-six years of misunderstanding
have been stitched in the cloak
worn by the daughter

loose threads hang from the garment
the daughter is careful not to pull
        not to tug
on mother's history
marked and saved for her.

Untitled

My mother dresses me in
gowns of guilt.
She stitches fear neatly
in the sleeves,
tucks shame inside the
facings.
The hem is laced with
madness.

Untitled

My child is gone.
i am like a check
that has been voided.

Cracked Glass

The cracked glass didn't cut me.
Damn it! Having a party and
dropping the champagne bottle
through the glass-top table,
is that any way to start a party?
The white snow gleamed. Below
zero it was, damn party probably
wouldn't get off the ground. And who is
this sweet young man in my apartment
yelling about symbolism? The spilling
champagne is red, pink. He keeps
yelling about symbolism and spilling
and shattering. If you're looking
for symbolism I want to say I'm in
my period. The right time of the
month. I should have cancelled
the party, said it was the snow. I
could go out and wash the white snow
with my red blood. I could stain the
white snow like I stain my sheets
that first night. All the red.
All the red in the house, people
keep talking about red. And someone
at my own party tells me I look like
a tainted lady. Tainted. A red
Indian print skirt on and a red flower
in my hair, red champagne, red
menstrual blood and shattered glass
splintering my nerves. The table breaks
before the guests arrive. The center
cannot hold.

Dreams

I dream of roller coasters, crashes,
supposed to be scary but they're not
Even poisonous peas taste good.

Dope Man

The dope man runs fast
Got a lot of stops to make he says
his black coat and hollowed eyes show his secrets
i realize
i've never seen his eyes before
when you look at him
you see yourself.

Untitled

The train dances along
shifting its weight
from left
to right
steady rhythm
speeded up
to the tune of rumble music
vibrations
A whistle

Corn and beans and telephone
poles — a small white
farmhouse in the
distance flanked nicely
by trees — swaying
cows graze
and old tree trunks
bleached like driftwood
are poised with a branch
up in the air

7-Up, the Trojan Drive-in —
A custard stand. I think of
a rubber.
Grain bins looking like
silver penises ready to
pop their tops
corn
a farmhouse

Sanfran, Union Square

Old man, wearing gray hat
Lundstrom, the label reads

The planets are changing
the old man says
Pluto's coming back to his own
house, first time in 200 years

Uranus is in Scorpio now
might be in Sagittarius
I'll have to look it up
watery-eyed 75

My name's Sam, what's yours?
Say, I'll make out your horoscope
next time I see you I'll give it to you

Know the time? Take care of your
diet, then you'll be rich.

I'd give three thousand dollars
for a set of teeth like you've got
Went to get my teeth cleaned in 1924
Dentist killed all the nerves.

They didn't know what they were doing
back then ...

I'm from Poland. Had a dream to go
to America, saved my life. Parents
were exterminated. Worked in the shipyards
then my own business. Notions. Yardage.

Say, you need anything?
A coat?

You hungry? I'll feed you chicken
can get it for one forty-nine a pound
apples five pounds for a dollar you
got a mother and father?

Say, there are a lot of pigeons here today.

Untitled

I've taken all the insults
I can take on my car
the last a
sunny day
at a bank
drive up
where tellers
talk of the sound of
my $aab, warming
ummmm/ummmm/ummmm
I see them
laughing there
behind the glass
there is so
much to laugh at
no handles and
so I carry a screwdriver

Silhouette

Clouds — a floor of
clouds — you could
reach in, take a
handful of cloud,
wipe the cold cream from
your face.

The circle gets
big The rainbow
becomes a hoop The
shadow of the
plane flies through

Ann is reading a report
my ears
pop
The descent
takes the shadow
away

Rain

bounce and bubble
      dribbles
stomp hard and vibrant
      circles
     hop fast
     drops
here. no. here.
clear patterns this black
wet shiny night
i turn down my radio
to listen to your call

Dreams

we lie sleeping
he dreams of Galileo, Bach,
famous race car drivers explaining
mechanical functions

I dream of old clothes
A sleeveless
black and white tunic
the saleswoman encourages me
"take these clothes"
they don't fit
I protest
they're not my style
will someone listen?

Total Recall
we lie sleeping
he dreams of Galileo, Bach,
famous race car driver
explaining mechanical functions.

Spring Tune-up

Change my oil
check my plugs and points
give me a lube job
see my button
hot light flashing
        red

It's my thermostat
don't you smell
something's burning under there
open the hood
I need air and lots of water
        to run right

Cool me down first
I don't want my block to crack
watch my lid — protect yourself
come too close too fast — I burn and steam
        leave marks

Will you change my oil
smutty old stuff
eke it out drop by drop
replace it with fresh liquid
the best you've got
        please

First Night

you held me once and hold me still
the kids play in the attic
making their own house
It is Sunday outside the window
the hickory nuts fall fast.

Vachel's Place

There's a woman *in a blue dress.* Her cigarette
smoke spirals over your house.
The woman wears a dress the color of your steps
the blue ocean and teal.

Writers stand around smoking
"I wonder what was there before
the telephone company" one says wistfully
pointing across the street
Call Ma Bell

Would she know?

I was impressed with your house
VL. An old woman read poems for
your dining table the lace
tablecloth was oil when
shook together for a short while

And then separated

The needlepoint chairs were uncomfortable
spoked. Right now an Indian
leans on my shoulder. Passersby
peer out of their autos to see
what the cause for celebration on
your lawn is

dead stalks in those bushes?

One flower blooms. Fuzzy haired
women stand on your
porch, listen to sirens in the distance.

Essays

A Day in the Life

There's a story in everything that happens to me. In the past, I wasted my time and energy worrying about what would happen to me if my ideas dried up. But running out of ideas is the last thing I have to worry about. Ideas come where I least expect them.

Take Monday, for example. It started out to be a normal day, a day like any other. I had planned to dig around in my files and retrieve checks and receipts that could satisfy the IRS; I was undergoing an audit. I spent several hours digging into my piles and files and was much heartened to see that most of the checks and receipts did match up. I felt so good about this, I decided to go for a walk in the park. But before the walk, I returned four videos at Blockbuster and went grocery shopping at National.

As usual, I didn't have any money. I'm self-employed and I always have a cash flow problem. This makes me feel destitute and desperate. I've been listening to "Money Love" tapes and, like all new-age propaganda, I feel like my poverty is now my fault. I have poverty consciousness.

I bought Bumblebee tuna at National because I was preparing to join Weight Watchers, a thought that horrified me. I selected the best-looking broccoli, which was a hard task because all the broccoli was limp. One large hard green pepper. Green onions. I contemplated chicken parts. Whole or half? Boneless or boned? Breasts or thighs? I bought an itsy bitsy teeny weeny loaf of pumpernickel bread from the bakery. I strolled and shopped and shopped and strolled and even prevented a disaster with a small child and a full grocery cart. At the checkout counter, I lamented the 79-cent price I paid for the green pepper.

Then I drove to the park. When I entered the park, I saw a man whose behavior looked suspicious. He kept turning around, looking, like he'd done something wrong. I ignored him and opened the trunk of my car so I could put all the cold and frozen foods together in one bag while I did my walk. It was warm in the park, and even warmer in my car. I walked with my Walkman, noticing the blue sky. The sky, I thought, was the best reason to live in Illinois — and maybe the only. I watched the ducks and ducked the cars. I noticed that in the park, even pigeons don't look as ugly as they really are.

After I completed a round in the park, I went back to my car — which I had parked at the lagoon — and drove home. When I went to get my groceries out of the back, they were gone. My trunk was unlocked; I didn't slam it hard enough.

I was furious. Someone had stolen my food. Twenty dollars. I felt victimized and violated. How dare someone enter my car and take the groceries I had spent time and money shopping for? I wouldn't do that to someone else. The nerve.

Immediately, two voices in my head started warring with each other. "If someone stole your groceries, he must need them more than you do." Since I was broke, the other voice said, "No. That's not true. Who knows if the thief was even hungry? Maybe some wild teens stole them and fed my Bumblebee tuna to the ducks."

Fortunately, my strong voice won. "You've been ripped off," it said. "Don't think about the criminal. Think about the victim. You wouldn't open another person's car and steal his groceries. Get mad. Get your groceries back. Call the police. Go back to the park. It's an eye for an eye."

I called the police and they asked if I wanted to file a report. I thought about it, but I figured the $10,000 the IRS said I owed them versus the two hours I'd spend with police for $20 was not a good trade-off. Besides, I wouldn't get my groceries back.

So I had no one to talk to, no one to tell. The police should hire empathetic trained counselors to appease crime victims, I thought. They should set up shooting ranges where victims could go and relieve our anger by bombarding cardboard figures with bullets. They could have a cardboard assailant for every crime; one could be carrying my groceries.

This crime made me think about the other two crimes of which I have been a victim. I got mad about those two all over again: the time my stereo was stolen and the time I was held up by a masked gunman who blindfolded me and took my money.

These crimes made me think about writing articles on crime. How many robberies occur in this city each year? How many offenders are caught? How many are prosecuted? How many are convicted? How many cop a plea?

Thinking about stories about crime made me think about the IRS. Until my audit, I didn't know it was possible to terrorize the IRS. My accountant said it was not a good idea because the IRS could terrorize you. Other people had told me stories about their audits — how they dumped three years of receipts on the agent's desk and told him to figure the mess out. How they carried in brown paper grocery bags stuffed with receipts and dug around in them all day looking for particular receipts the agent requested. How they jerked the IRS around until the statute of limitations was up and they didn't have to pay a thing.

Were these stories true, I wondered. Wouldn't it be fun to interview IRS agents and accountants and the guys who made up these stories? "How I Screwed the IRS" was an article that could find a market. I'd write it myself, but I was too busy wading through my two files, labelled "stuff" and "miscellaneous." Maybe I could write an article about my audit. I already had the title: "I Fought the Law and the Law Won," the old song by Bobby Fuller.

In between stolen groceries, crime victim flashbacks and the IRS audit, I had car trouble. The car stalled in traffic, of course, on a busy street. As bad as I felt spending $20 on groceries, I felt 10 times worse spending $125 on a car. Something in the carburetor.

I gave the mechanic my only car key and told him it was my only key. He lost it and five guys, the regulars who hung out at the station, spent an hour looking for it. The station office was in such disarray it reminded me of my financial records. One of the guys found the key next to my mechanic's car in the parking lot.

There's a story here, I thought. Why do some people have extras of everything and others live life on the edge — one key for one car? Actually, I had a reason for having only one key but if I went into that now, you would miss the chance to hear about my photograph albums. Along with organizing my receipts for the IRS, I'd been organizing my life in pictures — a task that had taken me weeks. Not only was time involved, but emotional trauma was involved too.

I started at the beginning: the few photos I had of my family before I got married and had children. Mom, Grandma and my two sisters. I moved on to life before marriage — proms and trips. Life during marriage was another album. Everyone looked unhappy, especially me. Life after marriage got a little more interesting — life on Park Street, life in California, life on Washington Street, life on South Grand.

Later I scrapped these titles and retitled the albums. "I Work at the Bank." "My Sister Gets Married." "Two Sweet Babies Are Born and Photographed. And Photographed." "Should This Marriage Be Saved?" "The Kids Join the Day-Care Co-op." There's a story in every photograph: mood, event, space, time, place.

I relabelled the vacation album "Florida and Some Pennsylvania." I relabelled the "Life on South Grand" album to read "London, Paris, New York City and the Special Ed Prom." "The Gradual Destruction of Downtown Springfield" was another relabelled album. And another story. It wrenched my heart to see my town the way it used to be.

After surveying my work and putting photos away, I went to Weight Watchers. By this time, I was happy. My albums were in order. The sun was out. My receipts and checks were matching up nicely. Life could get better.

But not at Weight Watchers. I thought I was in a depression clinic. Everyone looked unhappy. I was weighed and given a card. A recipe for diet French toast was on the board. I wrote it down even though I knew I'd never fix it.

There were 50 women and no one said a word to me except one man who had lost 100 pounds. He was thin now and there was some comfort in that. He told me the secret of Weight Watchers in one sentence: "Write down everything you eat and drink all your water." It sounded so simple.

"Is that all?" I murmured.

The workshop leader talked down to us. Women blamed themselves for their losses or victories. No one asked the question I came to debate: Why do we want to be thin anyway? Doesn't this fat protect us? I thought there was a story there. Actually, I could think of several reasons for staying fat — the main one being that when I'm fat, I don't buy many clothes so I save money.

But I didn't want to be disruptive the first day. I had a feeling that no one in the group would share my desire to debate a question so basic. And the women were getting red ribbons for losing 10 pounds. And I decided I did want to lose weight. And I hoped I could write everything down and drink my water. Both prospects sounded dull and dreary. But maybe I would find a story.

If I Had Money

If I had money ...

I'd buy a double bed frame to put my mattress on so I wouldn't have to creep around on the floor changing the sheets.

I'd buy a new iron so I could discard the $3.50 one I bought at SalArms, which sticks to all my clothes even after I clean it.

I'd buy a vacuum cleaner that actually picks up, because my big sister once told me I'd like vacuuming if I had a cleaner that worked. (I don't believe her, but I'd like to give it a try, just to see.)

I'd buy a toaster oven that toasts both sides at once. The one I have is a SalArms special and it only toasts one side at once. (Never buy appliances at thrift stores — it doesn't pay.)

I'd buy a sturdy kitchen table (I have a borrowed formica one with one leg broken) and I'd buy a new sofa so I wouldn't get stuck by a broken spring when I am in compromising positions.

I'd buy a clothes dryer so I wouldn't have to hang clothes in the basement where they never dry, although it's wonderful hanging out in the summer.

I'd buy an Oriental rug, or maybe several.

I'd buy a tape recorder. I bought one once and it was stolen from my apartment along with my stereo, speakers, diamond ring — all I had. No apartment insurance. The Hard Way.

I'd buy furniture for my dining room, which is completely bare. But if I really had money, I'd have the room mirrored and install a ballet barre. I'd take ballet three times a week instead of one. I'd buy leg warmers and a ballet sweater and I'd send away for a Capezio catalog and order everything in it that I wanted.

I'd hire a teacher to come to the home and give my son ballet lessons. (His father and stepmother would never approve of a boy taking ballet. Also, he has coordination problems. That's not why they wouldn't approve; that's why I'd give him ballet.)

I'd never clip coupons and wouldn't hassle with prices at the grocery store.

I'd buy a pound of coffee and not feel bad about it.

I'd buy a carton of clove cigarettes and good wine.

I'd buy a whole outfit at one time: sweater, pants, skirt, jacket, blouse, shoes, purse, coat, scarf, hose, pants, slip.

I'd buy a down jacket, because I've never had one and they look warm. I'd buy Calvin Kleins and Glorias instead of SalArms and Goodwill specials.

I'd buy a new pair of jogging shoes because Anastasia took mine and I never got them back and now they're worn out.

I'd buy Madame Alexander dolls — and a dollhouse for Anastasia, even though she's too old this year.

I'd have a big holiday party and give out copies of Mary Daly's *GynEcology* to all the women I know, and some of the men if they'd promise to read it.

I'd buy the secretaries presents for the holidays and go over the $3 gift exchange limit.

I'd buy all the Beatles albums and play them all, but first I'd have to buy a component stereo set.

I'd leave the Midwest in the winter and go somewhere warm so I could come back with a suntan.

I'd buy books and health food and fly to Sanfran for a cup of cappucino or Newport for jazz and lobster.

I'd go to the race track every weekend and bet on the horses.

I wouldn't get furious when I lose $3 in poker games.

I'd see the reflexology expert every week and I'd go to a doctor who could dissolve my gallstone by medicine instead of surgery.

I'd pay the dentists $3,400 to rebuild my mouth so my smile wouldn't be crooked and wrinkles would go away from the right side of my mouth where it slopes unevenly.

I'd buy a Mercedes. (Right now I just go to the showrooms and sit in them. I like the smell of rich new cars. I drive a 1972 Impala and am currently paying $25 a month for it.)

I'd buy a home with a fireplace.

I'd hire Alice from *The Brady Bunch* to live with me and watch the kid when I go out of town, as duty calls.

I'd buy my friend a kiln so she could pot, and I'd open a home for artists to come and live and work and share.

I wouldn't count the beers the women drink on Tuesday nights when we have writers' group at my house.

I'd join NOW and buy a subscription to *Ms*.

I'd buy a portable electric typewriter so I wouldn't have to pay $30 every month to rent one and after I do that, I only have $150 to live two weeks on — me and the kid.

I'd laugh at editors when they reject my manuscripts.

Stepmothers

Stepmothers are a disadvantaged group. They suffer from discrimination and prejudice. They are so easily hated, and rarely loved. What does the vision of stepmother conjure up in your mind? I see Hansel and Gretel walking through the woods with bread crumbs because their father's new wife wanted to get rid of them. Remember Cinderella? Who could forget? Stepmothers are evil. Fairy godmothers are good.

My mother and father were divorced when I was very young. I don't really remember him. Mother never said anything bad about my father, even though he was a drunk and a womanizer and a wife beater. However, I heard plenty about the woman he married after my mother divorced him. She was, I gathered at an early age, an evil woman. She was the reason my father no longer visited us; she was the reason he left us. I thought she must be awfully powerful, able to conjure up spirits and evil curses. When I saw the wicked woman and she even looked like a witch, my belief was cemented. Surely it must be true about stepmothers as a category. They must be the ugliest, most wicked, cunning, evil human beings. I hated them.

I was prepared to run the script for all it was worth. My ex-husband remarried and asked for custody of our son. My son was now living with another mother, a stepmother. I really did hate her at the beginning. She was one of those women who never had any children. What do we call those women? Cold bitches. I thought she was. I knew she had a degree in psychology and I figured she was just waiting to try a little behavior modification on my child. That made me chuckle. I was just dying for her to try it and hoped she'd fail as miserably as I did. I know what you're thinking, dear readers — what a bitch (me), eaten away with jealousy and revenge. I admit to both.

I called her names. (Yes, jealousy makes you stoop low, low.) I don't even know why I was jealous. I was glad someone had taken my ex-husband off my hands. Anyway, the stepmother loved cats, so behind her back I called her Cat Lady. I called her much worse to her face. I, in short, was not particularly fond of the old girl, and I thought she matched my vision of the "wicked stepmother" perfectly.

For about the first six months she lived with my child, she was a constant source of irritation to me — telling me how to bathe, feed and play with him. He was 7 years old when he went to live with Cat Lady and his father. As an infant, he had been sick for the first three years of his life. Essentially, I saved the child's life and here was this bozo, wearing her new mother-never-practiced-psychologist cap, telling *me* how to care for my son. I hated her. We yelled and screamed and slammed telephones in each other's ears.

I don't know what happened, or when. All of a sudden, I gleaned little pleasure from hanging up the phone on her and calling her Cat Lady. She stopped trying to tell me how to mother my child. I surprised myself when I bought her a beautiful necklace for Christmas. It was a necklace I had wanted to buy for myself — a moon and star on a dainty silver chain, imported from Mexico. The kids gave her the gift on Christmas morning. They gave their dad a pair of socks. She definitely got the best deal. We talked on the phone Christmas Eve, and I decided she was okay. She has a lot of responsibility and so do I. She has shared my responsibility.

Anyway, the upshot of this whole stream-of-consciousness Faulknerian monologue is to say that I really don't hate stepmothers any more, and sometimes I even try to understand them. I don't know how they do it. Raising a child you haven't had a history with — colic, infancy, terrible 2s, horrible 3s, kind of tolerable 4s, crying 5s — it must be an overwhelming experience to just have a child handed to you. And, well, this year, love a stepmother.

Nastiness Turned Simple-minded

Dear Gentlefolk:
I would like to take this opportunity to advise you of some of the things I am running into when reading business and technical writing. I know most of you out their have probly seen the same thing so I feel it is my expressed desire to tell you that some of the errors I see make me so upset that I visibly loose my composer. Are them errors real, or is these just nastiness turned simple-minded. I heard a New York teen use that expression recently so I thought I'd rank on it. I sometimes have the extreme desire two educate the public on these errors. I mean, you know, after all, this is our language and all and its all we got. Is grammar the scientific rules that treat the elements of our language or what? Was you planning on improving your grammar, or what?

Anyways, I become very flustrated when I begin reading business and technical correspondence. Like its how I make my living, man, so you know that means I like do it alot. I harbored the misteaken assumption that writers with MBA's, BMW's, and condos know that their are three two's in our language and two there's. But I was wrong. Watch youre language, I cry but it falls upon deef airs. I try to educate them in all aspics of the language.

Well you know what it feels like to get a letter that could have been better. We all have examples of letters we could parade before the nation and announce: Look At This One. We could all get into playing "one-up" when it comes to poorly written correspondence which we have been forced to read. I tell you it lowers my moral to read it. I try not to make misteaks either, but we are not talking about obscurity here, we are not talking about the use of the subjunctive mood of the verb, altho we should be talking about those things. We are not talking about the four qualifying functions adverbs serve, nor are we talking about tense, which can get hairy. Nosiree. We are taking about a sentence being a complete thought, a subject and verb that agrees in number, the use of two, to and too and (2). We are talking about alot used as two words, a lot, which it is. Although someone's grammar teacher once said: A lot is a plot of ground. There was one woman who knew language was to die for.

We are talking about the use of the apostrophe. I assumed that everyone knew we have and use apostrophe's in our language. I was told, by one student, that he was not allowed to use apostrophe's in his organization. "We never use them," was his direct quote. And later I saw that the dude wasn't lying. I saw a sign from his agency, printed and displayed throughout the state: "Buckle up. Its the law." Ain't it the truth? They really ain't using apostrophes. Nastiness turned simple-minded.

But just between you and me, I know a grocery store chain that should be using apostrophes, too. This chain announces a message to its customers on the bottom of the ticker tape: Your Important to Us. Not you're. Not you are. Your.

Well, what can I say? Its discouraging. We don't know our grammar rules which includes prepositions. But I got a cure for that one. If ya remember the tune Yankee Doodle and sing this preposition song (courtesy of Linda Ferreira Sloman and her grammar teacher in Blandinsville, Illinois), youll do well:

> About, above, across, after
> Along, among, around, at
> Before, beside, between, against
> Within, without, beneath, through
> During, under, in, into
> Over, off, of, to, toward
> Upon, near, for, from, except
> By, with, behind, below, down.

Well, I gotta go. If you have any questions about grammar, please do not hesitate to contact me. Or you can call the grammar hotline if youre state has one. Remember that its ok to end a sentence with a proposition. Hoping to hear from you soon, (Does this ending dangle?)

I remain. (No, I don't, I go with the letter.)

Rosemary F. Richmond
Not a blood relative of William Safire, but a watcher of the words, nonetheless.

A Very Fishy Story

My mom had a brunch. A bunch of people came and brought their kids. Everybody came in and the apartment was smoky, so we went to the park. We wanted to ice skate on the duck pond, without ice skates, just skate around.

When we got to the park, we saw a big fish in the duck pond. We tried to get it out. A man at the park asked us if we wanted him to help us, and we said yes.

I ran home and asked Mom for a container to put the fish in. She was busy talking to her friends. When she finally got around to listening to me, she still didn't hear me.

"Mom," I said. "We found a great big fish at the park. We want to bring it home and cook it."

"Okay," she said.

"I need a container, Mom."

Mom didn't want to be bothered, but she finally got me a green plastic dish pan. It was too small. I looked up at her.

"I don't think it's going to fit in there. I need something bigger. This is a really big fish," I said.

"Oh, it can't be *that* big. Take this. Put it in your wagon," she said.

You should have seen the way she patted me on the head and smiled. I think she was thinking of a minnow or a tadpole or a perch, the kind that washes up on the Chicago beaches or something. I knew she didn't know what I meant. This was a big fish, big and silver and ugly. The way she looked at me, you would have thought I was imagining it or something.

I ran back to the park and met the kids and we put the fish in the dishpan, but it was too heavy to carry. The fish was flopping out at both ends because it was too big for the pan. So I went back to the house to get my mittens because we didn't want to touch it. And I got the wagon, too.

We pulled the fish home, Zoe and me and Rolf and Jessica and

Bridget and Allen and J.B. Me and Rolf held the fish to keep it from falling out of the wagon.

When we got the fish home, we left it in the front yard by the steps, so all the people coming to the brunch could see it. They went upstairs to the apartment and asked everybody if they had seen the fish downstairs.

Soon everybody came down to see it, even Mom. She thought it was funny.

There was a photographer at the party, and she took a picture of us. She was going to send it to the newspaper. We were going to be famous.

After the party was over, things weren't so much fun. Mom made me get rid of the fish because it was ugly and smelly, and I found out that we wouldn't cook it.

I threw it in the trash can.

Our landlord came home and yelled at us to get that fish out of the trash. Mom got all upset and screamed at me. I cried because the fish was even smellier and too heavy for me to carry.

I didn't want to take it back to the duck pond. Alone.

Larry, the boy next door, and Bridget, my friend who helped me find the fish, helped me take it down the alley.

There was an old wagon in the alley with two wheels on the back of it and a rope tied up in the front. We put our mittens on and fished the fish out. Then we put it in the old wagon and took it down the alley. We dumped it in the alley and never saw it after that. I think it was burned.

Beach House for Bibliophiles: The Sylvia Beach Hotel

Curl up with a book. Listen to the ocean. Tell two truths and one lie about yourself to strangers while dining on baked chinook salmon, broccoli with pine nuts and double-rich brownies. Gather in a room that reminds you of the life, times and personality of your favorite author. Read advice, poems, prose and dreams that other guests have penned in the journal beside the bed.

The Sylvia Beach Hotel, an oceanfront bed and breakfast for booklovers, is the closest you'll find to an English seaside hotel in the states. It's quiet. There are no telephones and no televisions in the guest rooms. "I'm the only Cable you'll find around here," Gudrun (Goody) Cable, one of the owners of the Sylvia Beach, is famous for saying.

Goody Cable and Sally Ford, best friends since age 3, opened the Sylvia Beach Hotel on March 14, 1987; this was the 100th anniversary of Sylvia Beach's birthday. Sylvia Beach — literary patron and friend of American writers in Paris — owned and operated Shakespeare and Company, a Left Bank Parisian bookstore, from 1919 to 1941.

Beach, an American expatriate from Princeton, New Jersey, also financed the publication of James Joyce's *Ulysses*. In addition to lending books, money and emotional support to American writers, she introduced the "lost generation" of American and British writers to one another. Ernest Hemingway, Ezra Pound, T.S. Eliot, F. Scott Fitzgerald, Sherwood Anderson, James Joyce and Katherine Ann Porter all frequented Shakespeare and Company, the lending library that offered English-language editions and was a gathering place for the literati.

The daughter of two artists who met when they were students

at the Art Institute in Chicago, Cable was raised on art, music, literature and conversation. These are the things that are important to her, and she brings them together at the Sylvia Beach Hotel. In 1984, she and Sally Ford purchased the old Gilmore Hotel for $144,000 and had it declared a national landmark. Formerly an elegant 39-room resort, the Gilmore had spent years sliding from the honeymoon capital of the Oregon coast to a hotel for transients. Cable and Ford spent two and a half years remodeling the dark green structure — perched on a 40-foot cliff overlooking the ocean — and named it after Sylvia Beach.

They also hired an innkeeper, Ken Payton, who formerly managed 16 Wendy's restaurants in Montana. Payton, Sally Ford's brother, is the man at the desk and on the phone and the person with whom guests chat. Payton, a business major in college, says he always wondered what the philosophy and anthropology majors were going to do when they got out of school. "Now I know," Payton says. "They become entrepreneurs and hire business majors like myself to run their businesses."

Unlike most entrepreneurs, Cable and Ford are interested in art as well as profit. They invited their friends to decorate the rooms and to duplicate the atmosphere of Shakespeare and Company — a place where guests could read and converse. "A place where you wouldn't have to leave just when the conversation started to heat up," Cable says. In exchange for decorating, Cable and Ford gave each of their friends a week-long stay for the next five years. The decorators included a librarian, guitar maker, newspaper editor, TV personality, architect, private eye and arts critic.

There are three categories of rooms: classics, best-sellers and novels. One of the most popular classics is the Agatha Christie room. Decorated in green English chintz, it has a tiled fireplace and a walnut secretary. More than 80 clues from Christie's novels have been strategically placed in the room — a note on the secretary, a bottle labelled "poison," men's wing tip shoes protruding from under the drapes, wax on the rug, bullet casings imbedded in the wall and footprints on the window sill. Because the Agatha Christie room has an oceanfront view, a fireplace and a deck, it is considered a classic, as are the Mark Twain and Colette rooms.

One of the rooms in the best-seller category is the Tennessee Williams room, which is decorated in white wicker and adorned with a stuffed palm tree and parrot, reminiscent of *Night of the Iguana*. Pink mosquito netting surrounds the bed. A poster advertising *Streetcar Named Desire* hangs on the wall. Tiny glass figurines are placed on the wicker shelf. An eclectic grouping of quotes reminds guests of Tennessee: "I have always depended on the kindness of strangers." A collection of Tennessee's works are displayed on the desk. Former guests have written about wanting to finish reading *Memoirs* and having to leave while in the middle of the book. In the bedside journal, couples also have written about the ambience of the room and how it inspired romantic desires — steamy sex and mosquito netting entanglements are often mentioned. Still other guests have penned messages to Blanche in southern dialect.

One traveller, who has visited inns in Ireland, Germany, France, Austria and Holland, says the Sylvia Beach was like visiting abroad.

The Poe room is another best-seller, offering an ocean view from the window. Rumor has it that a couple once spent a honeymoon night in the Edgar Allen Poe room. Apparently, according to stories, the black wallpaper, the crimson velvet drapes and the mechanized pendulum that hangs over the bed did not disturb them. Nor did the stuffed raven that sits on the desk. Inside the closet is a brick wall from which the balled tops of Fortunato's fool's cap hang. *A Cask of Amontillado?*

One of the rooms categorized as a novel is the peachy pink Oscar Wilde room. Victorian wallpaper adorns this small room suitable for one person. "Either this wallpaper goes or I do," were Wilde's purported last words when he was dying in a Parisian hotel.

Virginia Woolf, although she does not have a room decorated in her honor at the Sylvia Beach Hotel, once said, "One cannot eat well, sleep well or love well unless one has dined well." The owners of the Sylvia Beach have taken this quote to heart and provide healthy, delicious fare in the Table of Contents Restaurant. Dinner is served family style at 7. Chapter 1 might be Mexican seafood salpicou; Chapter 2, tossed greens with curry dressing; Chapter 3, fresh garlic bread; Chapter 4, scallops aux blue cheese; Chapter 5, sautéed kale and summer squash with mushrooms; Chapter 6, sesame fettucine; and Chapter 7, lemon sponge custard.

During dinner, while seated at a table with strangers, guests are asked to play a game: two truths and a lie. The game has become a tradition and some of the truths and lies have become legend. One man said, "I once saw the pope naked." And it was the truth. He and his wife were in Venice, and he was in a hotel room taking a shower. His wife saw the pope and his entourage going by outside, so she called to her husband to come to the window. He did. And he saw the pope while he (the husband) was naked.

Another story that became a legend was from a woman who said a friend dared her to steal a chicken from a supermarket. The supermarket did not have a fresh chicken, so she stole a frozen one and put it under her hat. She had to wait in line a long time because the customer in front of her was having trouble cashing a check. The woman's head got so cold, she passed out. This was a lie.

While these stories are legend, Ken Payton has other favorite stories. He remembers two women who met because they were seated next to one another in the restaurant. One woman mentioned a little island where she had worked 52 years ago. The other woman, from Newport, had lived all over the world and had also worked on that same island at the same time. The woman from Newport ran home to get her photograph album and the two sat and chatted.

Goody Cable has achieved her goal of providing a haven for booklovers and a comfortable place for lively discussion. The Sylvia Beach is her second successful venture. In 1980, she and co-owner Phil Bass opened the Rimsky-Korsakoffee House in Portland, Oregon. At the coffee house, classical music is a backdrop for intellectual conversation. A life-size Eric Satie supposedly reclines in a bathtub upstairs. To finance Rimsky-Korsakoffee, Cable wrote a book, *Quotidian*, a calendar of quotations. While she read, she kept running into Sylvia Beach's name. When Cable and Ford opened the hotel, they had the perfect name for the place.

In a way, Goody Cable is like Sylvia Beach. She inspires the creativity of others and even assists them in their efforts. It is not unusual to find artists and writers waiting to talk with Goody. But, according to Payton, some people think the Sylvia Beach is for writers. It's not, he says. It's for readers. And the avid readers come to the hotel. Some guests book a year in advance. The Sylvia Beach Hotel, formerly the Cliff and Gilmore hotels, has come to life again.

How to Get Along Without a Car

Wear plastic boots when it rains. Keep an umbrella in good working order. Make sure you have a long raincoat to cover your clothes; if you don't, two very large plastic garbage bags will do. Cut holes for the sleeves. You can even belt your bags if you want to be trendy. If you do not have something covering your business clothes while you wait at the bus stop in the rain, cars will splash you.

Hate the guy who drives up to the bus stop in a new Saab. His Saab has door handles and a cushioned interior. Hate him because your car repairs cost $500, more than your '74 Saab is worth. Even the Shadow (your mechanic) knows your car isn't worth fixing; you are not sure either. What you really want is a new Saab. What the guy at the bus stop has is a new Saab. Hate him on principle.

Try to rise above your pettiness while you wait in the rain for a bus. Listen to the rain. Meditate. Feel the wet drops. Watch your briefcase get wet. Fantasize about making a million dollars by inventing the perfect rainwear: Bus Stop Rainwear by Richmond, a loose-fitting plastic leotard complete with footies and headgear. Plastic briefcase covers. Imagine getting rich. Imagine hiring a chauffeur to drive you to work in a red three-block-long limousine. Remember that what you really want is a new Saab.

Enjoy getting wet. Pay attention to what it feels like to be really sopping wet. Remember that you have a cold. Think about getting pneumonia while waiting in the rain for the bus that never comes. Think about dying from pneumonia. Think about an end to car trouble. Think about something else. Remember that you are an extremist and dying is not the answer to car trouble.

Think about winning the lottery. Think about moving somewhere hot where it never rains. Think about luxury. Explore the idea of not working, of not worrying, of not walking, of not waiting for the bus.

Watch the woman on Spring Street have car trouble. Watch how she turns the key in the ignition and nothing happens. Wonder what the trouble is. Generator? Starter? Feel sorry for her. Turn away because you identify with her so much. It is so painful, you cannot watch. See her look helpless. Watch her get under the hood and look away helplessly. See her try to get the attention of another motorist. Notice the motorists blocked behind where her car is stalled; see how irritated they look. Be glad you are waiting for the bus. If the bus doesn't come, you can walk in the rain. You can dry off at the office. Realize that your feet have never failed you like your cars have.

Remember the car you had before this car. Remember "The Limo," the '73 Chevy, with the choke that would stick at the most inopportune times. Think about all the times you had to get out in the traffic to open the massive hood and unstick the choke with a pencil. Remember the day you did it while wearing a navy blue wool business suit and a Goofy hat you forgot you had on. Recapture the feeling of embarrassment.

Look down the street for the bus. Get anxious again. Get nervous because the other stops are empty; you are the only person waiting for the bus. Worry about whether the bus stops here, whether it has come and gone. Wonder why you are not the type of person who checks the bus schedule before she waits in the rain for 20 minutes. Speculate on how it is that you think you can gauge the bus's arrival by intuition.

Get excited. See something large coming. Hope for a bus. A large, warm, dry bus. Watch the water seep into your yellow Calvin Klein sandals. Wonder about a person who wears sandals in the rain to wait for the bus. Realize that you are not a practical person. Tell yourself you have known this for a number of years, but it does not seem to help.

Get depressed. Find out that the bus is not a bus. The vision becomes a reality. The imagined bus is a truck. Peer down the road. Try to see beneath the sheets of rain that rhythmically fall, like drumbeats, on your head. Watch the important papers in your briefcase get wet.

Realize that your umbrella is broken. Recognize that it is bent and the spokes are sticking out. Feel sorry for yourself. Think about the only umbrella you ever owned that you liked. Remember it was from Chinatown — San Francisco. It was paper and wood. You lost it in a bar. You always mourned it. It cost $5.

See a large vehicle down the road. Stifle your excitement. Try to act like you can handle it even if it is not the bus. It is not. It is a large van.

Get accustomed to waiting in the rain. Sing. Think of Gene Kelly: "I'm singing in the rain, just singing in the rain ..." Sing that song for a while. Smile. Act like your feet are not wet. Act like you don't hate your fellow and sister motorists. Act like you are not a resentful, jealous, petty person.

Tell yourself you are self-indulgent. Tell yourself there are important events going on in the world and you are only a small fly swimming in the cosmic soup. Tell yourself it doesn't matter if you get wet, and in the Zen of life, if one waits for a bus and longs for it, the bus will not come. A watched bus never arrives.

See a young man appear at a bus stop down the street. See him wait. Look hopefully down the street. Know that your efforts are not in vain. The bus will come. It does stop here. Watch the enormous vehicle trundle down South Grand, lights blazing.

See the bus stop for him. Watch how he shakes the rain from his umbrella before he boards the bus. Think about how polite that is. Think about how you never thought of it. Wonder if you are selfish and insensitive. Try to do what he does when the bus stops for you. Forget that your umbrella is broken and it is not as easy to open and close. Do it anyway. Make the bus wait. Get on. Ride to work. Think about how wonderful the bus is. Realize that if you hadn't suffered, you would never have known the joy of riding the bus.

When you arrive downtown, notice all the parking spaces in front of the office. Think about how you could have parked there; be disappointed. Remember the number of parking tickets you usually have. Get excited that you are on foot and the city cannot ticket you for walking and busing. Think about never driving again.

Get angry when you realize what they have done to the parking meters — how one quarter does not now net you one hour. Think about the pending lawsuit against the city. Realize how much more you will pay in parking tickets to finance something you don't believe in. Compose letters in your mind to the members of the City Council. Fantasize about a tea party on the lawn of the municipal building — like the Boston Tea Party. Protest taxation without representation.

Calculate how many parking tickets you would have to pay to arrive at $600,000. Speculate whether the lawsuit will cost $600,000 or $2 million. Realize that is a lot of parking tickets. Vow to take the bus. Sell your car.

The Artful Punster

David Hammons said "yes" to Springfield and "no" to Whitney Museum in New York City. The Illinois State Museum will show Hammons's works in an upcoming exhibition, *David Hammons: Hometown*, September 11 through November 8.

Hammons, who was born and raised in Springfield and will return to town this week from Rome, Italy, has family, friends and fans who eagerly await the event. No one knows what to expect, but everyone expects the unexpected.

How is it that Hammons, who describes his art as falling "somewhere between Marcel Duchamp, Outsider Art, and Arte Povera" ("poor art" created from everyday materials), turned down an invitation to participate in the 1991 Whitney Biennial? "I couldn't wait to tell 'em no," Hammons proclaimed in an August 1991 *Los Angeles Times* article by Amel Wallach. "Their relationship with black artists has been negative since Day One."

About the art world in general, he has said, "I know all the tricks and I ain't playing them."

Hammons doesn't have to play anyone else's games. For more than 20 years, he has followed his own interests, paid attention to the process of creating art and targeted his preferred audience. He has been labelled a conceptual artist, environmental sculptor, social commentator, performance artist, magician, poet, trickster and hip junk dealer. Hammons disturbs, upsets, criticizes and pokes fun at the "system."

He has created his own countersystem, eliminating his need for money and expensive art materials. He sees the world through his own lens. He creates his own space (outdoors and outside "The White Cube," or gallery world), courts his audience and shares his gift: creating, defining, reconstructing, reclaiming and empowering. Now, the art world he ignored is courting him.

Although Hammons now spends most of his time in Rome, the streets of Harlem were his longtime studio, the people on the streets his preferred audience. In Harlem, he fashioned art from objects he found: hair, eggs, chicken wings, spare-rib bones, paper bags, wine bottles, bottle caps, broken records, rubber inner tubes, fan blades, cigarettes, coal and grease.

But in the beginning, before performances on the streets of New York City, before notoriety, before installation art, there was commercial art and advertising, which Hammons studied in Los Angeles, where he moved in 1963 from Springfield. He studied at Los Angeles City College, Los Angeles Trade Technical School and later at Otis Art Institute and the Choulnard Art Institute. Advertising taught him how to develop an idea and invent the visual equivalent. Hammons honed his ability for the visual pun.

During the late '60s, Charles White was Hammons's mentor; White was a social realist whose works depicted the lives, struggles and pride of African-Americans. In the 1960s and early 1970s, Hammons's first works were prints, many of which used the American flag as a "symbol of America's unkept promises to and violence against African-Americans."

He also made body prints by greasing his own flesh and pressing it against paper. Fascinated with the word "spade," Hammons pressed his body in playing card shapes of spades, then dusted the impression with pigment. The result: Hammons appears ghostlike in shades of gray on black paper.

The prints were popular and Hammons made money; however, he became more interested in pursuing the spade symbol. By 1973, Hammons had created spade forms: he adorned the head of a shovel with chains and turned it into an African mask.

In *Rousing the Rubble*, the catalogue from his retrospective, Hammons said, "I was trying to figure out why black people were called spades, as opposed to clubs. Because I remember being called a spade once, and I didn't know what it meant. 'Nigger' I knew, but spade I still don't. So I just took the shape and started painting it. I started dealing with the spade the way Jim Dine was using the heart. I sold some of them. Stevie Wonder bought one, in fact. Then I started getting shovels/spades. Outrageously magical things happen when you mess around with a symbol. I was running my car over these spades and then photographing them. I was hanging them from trees. Some were made out of leather. I would take that symbol and just do dumb stuff with it, tons of dumb, ignorant, corny things. But you do them and after you do all the corny things, then a little bit of brilliance starts happening. There's a process to get to brilliancy."

On to Mecca

Hammons left Los Angeles in 1974 for New York City to "run

with the big boys." "If you're a true pilgrim, go to Mecca," he has told young artists he mentored at the Studio Museum in Harlem. This was part of his process and part of his brilliancy. He combed the streets of Harlem for scraps and discards, found richness in ruins and began working with grease on paper bags and African-American hair.

Greasy Bags and Barbeque Bones appeared in Just Above Midtown Gallery in New York (1975). Hammons controlled the saturation of grease on discarded paper bags and decorated the bags with spare-rib bones, glitter and hair. Although hair was used for decorative purposes in this series, it was the next element he chose to explore.

For five years, Hammons worked with hair. He made quilts by stuffing hair into metal screens. He attached hair to wire, used hair as a wallpaper pattern. "Those pieces were all about making sure that the black viewer had a reflection of himself in the work," he said.

In an interview with Robert Starr, curator of the Museum of Modern Art in New York City, Hammons said, "I first saw hair on some African sculpture in the Chicago Art Museum and I decided that was the essence of African culture. You look at that hair. No one can have that hair unless you're African. That was my common denominator to making purely African art. People of color have woolly hair."

In the '80s, Hammons's obsession turned to basketball and he turned telephone poles into ornate totem poles topped with basketball hoops. He erected a series of poles, entitled *Higher Goals*, and adorned them with thousands of beer bottle caps, fashioned into Islamic designs. "It's an anti-basketball sculpture," he explained. "Basketball has become a problem in the black community because kids aren't getting an education. They're pawns in someone else's game. That's why it's called *Higher Goals*. It means you should have higher goals in life than basketball."

"I'm enraged with basketball," said Hammons, who averaged 30 points a game as a guard for Edison Junior High School in Springfield, 1957-58. "I played it growing up, six, seven hours a day. It wasn't about height then. When it became all about being tall, it took me out of the game. This is my revenge."

Snowballs and Doll Shoes

That is Hammons being serious; he is also funny. In the 1983 New York blizzard at Cooper Square, Hammons performed *Blizaard Ball Sale*. He lined up snowballs in neat rows, from small to large, and sold them. He made $20. Two years later, he performed

Doll Shoe Salesman, where he arranged and rearranged doll shoes in patterns on the street. Consumers bought the shoes for 50 cents a linear foot.

In November 1989, Hammons received national attention for his 14 by 16-foot metal cutout of Jesse Jackson in white face, with blond hair and blue eyes. "How Ya Like Me Now?" Hammons called to his audience in Washington, D.C., where the piece was installed. Black viewers responded with sledgehammers, partially destroying the portrait. Jesse Jackson viewed the damage and called the work "inoffensive." "Sometimes art provokes. Sometimes it angers," Jackson said. "That is a measure of its success. Sometimes it inspires creativity. Maybe the sledgehammers should have been on display too."

Hammons took Jackson's advice. He now shows the piece ringed with a fence of sledgehammers, one handle festooned with a Lucky Strike cigarette wrapper. According to Hammons, the attack was "a lucky strike," because it netted him international publicity (which he read about while in Italy). Hammons did not view the attack as destructive. "They didn't smash it. They anointed it," he said.

Grease. Hair. Basketball. Wine bottles. And jazz. At Exit Art in Soho (1989), Hammons laid rusted railroad track upon which a model train, painted blue, ran through a landscape of upended baby grand piano lids. The train disappeared into a tunnel under a mountain of coal. Music accompanied the train as it circled: John Coltrane's (Coal Train?) *Blue Trane* album, James Brown's *Night Train* and works by Thelonius Monk. David Hammons's voice called, "All aboard." The train was a metaphor for the Underground Railroad, the Freedom Train, the A-Train, the 4, 5 and 6 subway trains and the wrong side of the tracks. Sights and sounds, tracks and trains, the play on words, the pun, the interplay between the title of his work and the materials he uses to create it — these are Hammons's calling cards.

During the same exhibit, Hammons constructed a circular glass sculpture from empty bottles of Night Train wine. For Hammons, these bottles have power and spirit because the lips of African-Americans have touched them.

Hammons's humor surfaced again in a two-part show at the Jack Tilton gallery in New York (1990). In one piece, Hammons used flags, oil cans and ice to install *Whose Ice Is Colder?* He hung three flags over washtubs filled with blocks of ice. The flags were South Korean, Arabic (Yemen) and American, although the American flag had been refashioned Hammons-style: stars and stripes in green, red and black, colors of black liberation. To understand the message, the viewer had to know there was a racial uproar among Arabic and Korean shopkeepers and black customers.

"When I go into the studio, all of the things that I see socially — the social conditions of racism — come out like sweat. My defense is to deal with racism and how racism is destroying our country," he has said.

For almost 25 years, Hammons has created thought-provoking elegant sculpture that comments on the problems of patronage and power, greed and neglect and patterns of the poor. While much of Hammons's works have been dismantled because of the impermanence of installation art, Tom Finkpearl managed to organize a David Hammons 22-year retrospective (1969-1990) at PS 1 Museum in Long Island City. The exhibition *Rousing the Rubble* featured Hammons's early works, including body prints, hairpieces, bottle sculptures, inner-tube wall pieces and a small sculpture of chicken wings as well as his more recent sculptures.

While most of his works have been inspired on the streets of New York, he also admits to being influenced by Antonio Gaudi, Marcel Duchamp, Federico Fellini and Simon Rodia.

Hammons is the recipient of many awards, including the American Academy in Rome Fellowship, a MacArthur Foundation Fellows Award (also called the Genius Award), a Guggenheim Foundation grant and a National Endowment for the Arts award.

He has been featured in major exhibitions, both in the United States and abroad. Recently he was featured in an eight-person show, *Dislocations*, at New York's Museum of Modern Art; in *Documenta 9* in Kassels, Germany; at Exit Art in New York; at the Studio Museum in Harlem; and at the Wexner Center for the Arts in Cincinnati.

Hammons uses his gift to transform the common to the sacred. Like a musician, his work can be delicate and whimsical; like a poet, punning or riddling; like a realist, evoking laughter, sorrow or anger. No one knows what David Hammons has planned for his installation at the Illinois State Museum, but plan to experience it.

This article was originally published in the September 9-15, 1993 issue of Illinois Times.

Hammons Comes Home

When I hear David Hammons is coming to town, I am excited. We were classmates at Lanphier High School in Springfield, Illinois. In 1962, he was the most interesting guy in the class, but it was difficult to connect with him. He didn't trust white people.

Before he arrives, I research his art career and write an article for the *Illinois Times*, Springfield's weekly newspaper. Then I bug the assistant curator of the Illinois State Museum, Bob Sill, until David shows up in the flesh.

When I approach David Hammons to introduce myself, he doesn't recognize me. I want to sing that old '60s tune, "You don't remember me, but I remember you." I remember anyone who escapes from Springfield.

I am impressed by his gentle manner and spiritual essence. In high school, he was sensitive and silent. Today, he wears colorful African garments — purple and white, patterned with birds — and a multicolored leather hat from Jamaica. He has eyes you can see the world through.

He stands in the museum space, tells me he has to go home for a couple of boxes, asks if I can wait for half an hour to talk with him. I've waited 30 years, I think.

He returns with two boxes of materials: gold chains, yo-yos, dentures, an African mask, elephant dung, rods which he sharpens on a file. "It's sad to be in a town where you are older than the buildings," he says. I agree. It's sad to be in this town anyway, but I don't say it. He might ask why I'm still here. Besides, the buildings are a big loss. Especially the six movie theaters. Everything David remembers is gone, except the house he grew up in. "The rooms in that house get smaller every time I visit. That house was so little, I had to go outside to have an opinion." He arranges elephant dung and mouse turds on a silver platter. "Know what this is?" he asks.

"Looks like big shit, little shit to me," I say.

"These are the senators," he says, pointing to the elephant dung. "And these are the masses." He points to the mouse turds.

We laugh. I think about where I am — Springfield, Illinois, the state capital, the legislature within a turd's throwing distance and the politics like excrement.

Museum staff comment on the beauty of the African masks. "People used to tell me to go back to Africa. That's what I was told as a child. I didn't even know where Africa was. I'd like to go back to Africa. Then they'd say, 'Yankee, go home.'"

He studies the empty room. A photographer from the local paper shoots pictures. I ask a question every now and then. Is the house on Second Street still there? "Yes," he says. "Memorial Hospital wants to buy it. All the property owners are fixing up their houses, hoping the hospital will buy. I ought to buy it. Turn it into a museum."

I encourage him to do that.

"Abe Lincoln already filled up all the space in this town." He takes a drink of LaCroix.

I leave to sell insurance.

When I return, David is filing copper rods. The assistant curator asks if he can help. "Thought you'd never ask," Hammons says, and gently trains him in the Hammons filing system.

When I come back on Wednesday, gold chains are being installed on a white wall in designs, like waves. One wall has been painted blue. I bring my yearbook, the *LHS Lan-Hi*, which I think makes me look like a major dork, but I don't want him to forget that once we were friends. While David works, the museum guard flips through the *Lan-Hi*. I want to show him David's picture, but he is busy looking at the women: "Look at the glasses these wimmens are wearing," he says to another guard.

Two walls have been painted — one red, one blue. The American flag, refashioned Hammons-style, hangs straight first, then at an angle. A stuffed peacock sits proudly above the flag. "I'm here to paint the town red," David says. Little Joe, a guy in a cowboy hat and red and white checked shirt, is doing the actual painting. When David's not around, Little Joe worries how many coats of white paint it will take to cover the red after David is gone.

The guard continues to look at the yearbook, laughs at people he knows, mentions their names out loud. A pallet with 20 bags of play sand sits in the middle of the floor. A pond is being built out of wood.

A volunteer makes a run for thin flat steel welding rods. David does not want to use the copper rods he has been filing. "Makes me feel like I'm doing something for the Holiday Inn," he says. It's the shine he objects to. Soft balls of African-American hair adorn the rods that were filed yesterday. A five-gallon glass jar holds a basketball. The opening of the jar is the size of a baseball. "How did you get that ball in the bottle?" someone asks. "Black magic," Hammons says.

I hang around the museum, looking at his treasures, wondering what he will create with clear plastic tubing, a bicycle pump, a mask, a sugar bowl, yo-yos, false teeth, zipper flies, a rusty rat trap, clumps of tangled chains.

The assistant curator says, "David, we really require your attention to build the pool."

But David has picked up my yearbook. I show him the Student Council picture; we laugh at our youth and innocence. Then he relives the racism he experienced. He points out "kids I ran with for 15 years." They abandoned him at puberty. "There's only one seat in a car," Hammons says. He tells me his brother was arrested for kissing a girl at Enos Park. I remember the story; she was Italian.

When he sees my photo in the yearbook, he remembers me. "You were pencil thin," he says, "and always had something to say about everything."

He signs my yearbook and we reminisce about Glen King, a young black man killed in Viet Nam. I ask David if he remembers how Glen rolled his eyeballs back so only the whites of his eyes showed. David remembers. He wants to know if a ceremony was held after Glen's death. He relives events from high school. We laugh at the funny ones. Then discuss racism. "Part of the American diet," David says.

"David, we really need your attention," the assistant curator calls.

I leave to sell insurance.

At 3:30, I return to meet my friend Ginny, a photographer. A.C. Hudgins, David's friend and agent, has arrived from New York. He affixes small balls of hair to steel rods. The assistant curator sits on the floor with a clump of gold chains, untangling and unclasping them. David arranges the chains on the wall in patterns of waves.

He continues to look at the yearbook, teasing me about seeing my picture every two pages. He is funny, light and airy.

And then serious. I am in tears when he talks about eating dinner at Maldaner's restaurant Tuesday night and how he had never been there before, and how he had to get sandwiches to go at Walgreen's when he was a kid because he wasn't allowed to eat in the restaurant. He talks about his bad memories of Springfield.

"So why did you come back then?" I ask. I tell him I am happy he is here, and I am sorry he is so sad about it.

His agent says he wanted to come here, but it is painful for him.

In the meantime, a volunteer offers sugar cookies she has baked because she found out, from David's sister, that his favorite foods are sardines and sugar cookies. Together? I wonder, but I don't ask. David lectures on art history while he installs the chains, then American history as he reflects on the exhibit next to his — American Indians behind glass. Downstairs on the first floor are animals behind glass. "Maybe you should ring the exhibit with sledgehammers," I offer.

Later, a volunteer tells me David said he would like to do an installation on an Indian reservation and put white people behind glass, talking on the telephone.

Before A.C. arrives, museum staff and volunteers offer to transport him from the airport to the museum. "Don't worry about A.C.," David says. "He'll find it." A.C. finds the Hilton Hotel in downtown Springfield; the museum is about six blocks away and he has to ask five people before he finds one who knows. The tourists are the only people in town who know the location of the museum.

A.C. continues to string balls of hair on steel rods. I untangle chains and break every fingernail I have unclasping them. A museum staff member tells a story about walking her dog and how a rottweiler scared the "bejeezus" out of her. David is bemused by the expression. "Haven't you ever heard that word before?" she asks him. He laughs. "Not in that particular expression," he says.

Hammons lectures on Jackson Pollock, Jesus and history. A stuffed cardinal is added to his objects. The pool is ready. Two inches of water are in the pool. David has found dead sweet gum trees on his walks through Springfield and has arranged them on the west side of the pool. I add a Japanese float I got in Oregon when I vacationed in August with a group of Lanphier High School classmates. I tell David the girls aren't politically correct, but I suspended my politics for a week. He asks A.C. if he can imagine Nelson Mandela saying that. I tell him I am not Nelson Mandela.

The Japanese float has picked up a leaf. Someone asks David what kind of furniture he wants, what kind of a chest of drawers. David says it would be nice to have couches around to make the room homey. I watch the museum staff wince. He places the large shell I gave him over the motor in the pool. He hangs a yo-yo from a sweet gum tree. The trees are surrounded with sand.

I leave to sell insurance.

When I return, David is installing the wires and hair on the wall. A.C. is painting a gold pattern on the walls with a roller; the effect looks like wallpaper, gold lines with circles. "Too bad you didn't bring your clothes. I once painted a jacket with this roller," David says. I go home, get my red silk Carole Little jacket; David rolls a gold pattern on it. I match the walls.

David fixes the trees. Two video crews film him while he works. The museum staff talks and laughs.

On one wall, a silver heart — Noventa Novena — from Rome, Italy, has been mounted. David rolls a basketball in red clay (from Georgia) and throws it against the wall until circular patterns surround the heart. The heart, A.C. says, is used at confession. Afterwards, they nail the heart to the cathedral wall. There are so many of them that they have thrown some out.

A.C. continues to add layers of chains to the pattern. David paints Jesus black. The paint is too shiny, he thinks. He considers a dulling spray. I suggest he add dreadlocks, since there is an abundance of hair on the table where he is painting. He points out how sensual the figure on the cross is, asks me what INRI means. I ask staff and volunteers. Someone says, "Jesus of Nazareth, King of the Jews."

David adds a little nappy hair to Jesus, tells me that was my idea. I think of how much I have contributed — my shell, my float and hair for Jesus. The yearbook. Thank you, Jesus, I say aloud, because being in the same room with David Hammons is like plugging into a spiritual battery charger. I can feel the voltage. The museum is full of love, laughter and community — three things hard to get in any museum, especially in Springfield, where you get cold tile floors, Indians and animals behind glass.

Me: What did the Buddhist say to the hot dog vendor?
David: What?
Me: Make me one with everything.
David: Why did Mickey Mouse get shot?
Me: Why?
David: Because Donald Ducked.

Thursday morning, before I go to work, I stop by the museum to see the action. The Sangamon State University Access 4 Television crew arrives to interview David; David is not at the museum. He works until early morning, parties and returns at noon the next day. I chat with the crew. I have already tried to interview David on my TV show, *Works in Progress*, but he is not receptive. He tells me he'll do it next time he's in town. The crew settles for footage of the installation-in-progress.

I eat spice cake for breakfast, courtesy of a volunteer. Then finally, I leave for work. It is hard to leave the museum, because the space feels warm and loving, particularly when David is there.

My boss awaits me, glares at me. I humor him, go to lunch, talk about his vacation to Disneyworld, imagine what David would say about Disneyworld. Can't wait to get back to the museum for a karmic fix.

When I arrive, I smell fresh wood and stain. Little Joe cuts boards; Phil, the preparator, stains them. The stain eats through one finger on Phil's glove. He wishes he could stay at the museum tonight, but he can't because his sister is getting married. Little Joe whistles while he pounds nails into the 1 by 10s; he is making an edge or platform around the pool, which has been constructed with 2 by 8s and lined with heavy plastic.

David has moved one mask that spits water into the pond. A museum staff member flips through the LHS yearbook, commenting on people she knows. "Look at the hairstyles. All the women have wavy bangs." David says, "All the girls looked like Mamie Eisenhower, the boys like Elvis."

The water spouting from the mask chases my Japanese float. Phil stains. Little Joe hammers. I write. The guard watches. A small room, enclosed by a partition, is home to a stone head with hair and a video of David Hammons taking the stone for a haircut at Thompson's barber shop in Harlem.

Fred the guard borrows the yearbook. Little Joe tells me his ideas about the installation. He wants to hang tinsel from the dead sweet gums, put in "red, yella and green Christmas lights."

Phil stains the edging red mahogany, wonders if David will like it. David returns with a person from the Art Institute of Chicago; he has had lunch with her. He shows her the video. The light is on the mask, the flag waves, the peacock watches. My red jacket hangs on the red wall, matches the gold designs. The wires and hair cast shadows.

It is Thursday, September 9. David hammers steel rods adorned with clumps of hair onto the wall. A.C. continues with amber waves of chains. I think an installation could be done to "America the Beautiful," with the Hammons twist. Everyone in the museum has a camera except me. I have a pencil and a found pad. Three people video David while he works. I drink a beer from a large plastic cup with a moose on it, courtesy of A.C. via the assistant curator.

Fred the guard brings a copy of the *Illinois Times*. I borrow the arts section to see my article about David. He asks me to read aloud while he hammers and A.C. chains. I sit on a folding chair in the middle of the small room and read. When I'm finished, David says he will put a copy in the Schaumburg museum; A.C. says it is well-researched. Someone asks if David means Schaumburg, Illinois. He doesn't; it is in Harlem.

Ginny asks David if she can put his photo on pins and magnets. He questions why Americans want to sell everybody as a commodity. "Everybody wants to celebrate everything. This is not about celebration," he says.

He won't be interviewed for a video, won't pose for photos, won't allow himself to be a product. He talks of greed, redefines what the golden rule really means: he who has the gold makes the rule.

I sit on the floor, write, drink beer, feel guilty about not working. Jazz plays. People stroll through the installation-in-progress. The cameras roll. David puts up and takes down a muslin garment on the wall opposite the chains. The flag blows.

At night, David holds the stuffed cardinal. "Very beautiful," he says. "That's why people hate animals. They're not that beautiful." Ornette Coleman plays. David hammers, talks about recording street sounds in Germany. The water spurts. Drumsticks float in the water along with an empty bottle of LaCroix. He bends the wires and attaches them to the red wall with gold designs. The shadows from the wire sculptures look like delicate basketball hoops.

David changes the tape to Burning Spear. Says the young reggae musicians don't have the same spirit. Tells me Michelangelo started with the elbow when he carved marble. That's how familiar he was with his material.

The assistant curator calls Norb Andy's to see if we can be served dinner at 10 p.m. A.C. is hungry. I ride with the assistant curator and David downtown. David runs into his nephew. He orders chili and is disappointed. He adds mustard, ketchup and sour cream to make it edible. "I don't know how they could screw up chili," he says. "But they did."

He orders potato chips. He likes Norb's, asks me why he never saw the inside of the place before, wants to know how long it has been here. I tell him we were in high school; I never hung out at Norb's until I was in my 20s. He was in Los Angeles. The waitress gives him the menu, which has the history of the building; it has been in Springfield 56 years. David talks to his nephew, who sits behind us. He pays the tab.

We go back to the museum, drink wine, look things over. He asks me about the party after the opening. He "dreads" the opening.

On Friday, after working the morning, I arrive at high noon. The video crew from the Art Institute asks if I will be interviewed; they want me to talk about David's work. I check with him first. "I wouldn't want to say the wrong thing," I tell him.

"I don't care what you say," he says.

The exhibit looks finished. I hate to see it completed. At home, I get a call from a woman who says she grew up with David. She called him at the museum. "He was the sweetest guy," she says. "Mild-mannered and different." She says she once asked him if he carried a switchblade. I am embarrassed. She wants to know where she can get a copy of the yearbook; she didn't finish high school.

Ginny calls. She has a photo of David; she thinks he might like it. She invites me over to see it. We go back to the museum. Ginny has captured David's eyes and his smile. He keeps the photo with the softer matte finish, gives me the glossies.

"David," Ginny says. "If you could just move into the light for three seconds, I can get a shot without a flash." David says no. "It would be posed and therefore have no spirit."

"David," I say, moving as close as I can get to him. "You want me to write an article as a friend." I place my arm on his back. "Can you turn around so we can get a photo together?"

"You used to do this to me all the time and scare me to death," he says.

"Really?" Ginny asks. "She did that to you in high school?"

"Scared me," he repeats.

"Was she a wild woman?" Ginny asks, eager to prolong the conversation because she finally has a photo opportunity — his face. Everyone else has his back.

"Something's happening here," he says to himself as he prepares to hang slips on the wall where the muslin garment once stood — six slips, one for each sister. I hold the straps of the slips while he hammers a push pin to create a small hole, then uses a tiny gold nail. "When you have six sisters, every woman you go out with reminds you of some part of them." He bought the slips at the Salvation Army. He is not pleased that they are polyester, but he is pleased that the Salvation Army is so clean, that items are tagged and coded. Chains and slips, slips and chains. Slipping out of chains, I think.

David rearranges the African mask at the pool. "I call this piece 'Spitting Image,'" he says. He has decided to add fish to the pond.

The kids will like the fish, he thinks. A.C. and I go fishing. Aquaria Unlimited is out of business; so is the pet shop at the mall. A customer in the Mustard Seed, a religious bookstore, says we can find fish at WalMart. A.C. buys 12 goldfish, which die two hours after they are put in the pool. I think if we want the ring of authenticity, we should get channel catfish.

The museum group goes to Maldaner's — three museum staff, one husband, David, A.C., Calvin Reid and two crew members from the Art Institute Video Data Bank. David rides with me. My car is old but it doesn't bother him. "I can't deal with cars," he says. He doesn't own one. I have just moved my office, and the back seat of my '81 Toyota is filled with change-of-beneficiary forms, wastebaskets, telephones, IRA booklets, bond-fund brochures.

During the ride to the restaurant, David says, "Some of the streets here are brick, which is very nice. Very beautiful."

At Maldaner's, A.C. talks to Kate, the video woman, about the stock market. I talk to the other crew member about women in the sex industry and violence against women. The husband of the museum staff member talks about restoring the Frank Lloyd Wright Dana Thomas house; he offers a personal tour to A.C. and David. David toasts the assistant curator and predicts he will lose his job because of the exhibit.

Back at the museum, after dinner and cognac, we drink wine, clean up the rubble. I gather my rocks and shells, fishing twine, my jacket.

When we leave, David, A.C. and Calvin want to ride in my car, but I only have room for one. David says he'll make room for himself in the back seat and he shoves forms and phones around until he can squeeze in. "Looks like a homeless person's car," he says. "You could live in here." I tell him I loved his drawing in *Rousing the Rubble*, "Homeless Ain't Home." I don't tell him it made me cry.

David is still ready to party. A.C. gives me money for more fish. David says, "No goldfish that are gold."

Saturday morning, the Fish Man is open for business at 10 a.m. I buy four gray goldfish and one Japanese Koi — it's orange and black, our school colors. I get to the museum; there is no one working except the guard. Two visitors tour the exhibit: a young African-American man and his daughter. He says he read the article in the *Illinois Times* and couldn't wait to see the exhibit. His daughter likes the fish.

The museum guard says someone wrote a note to the assistant curator complaining about the Hammons exhibit. He says veterans are complaining about the flag and many people are reacting to Jesus.

Saturday evening, the museum hosts the reception for the artist. Usually 250 people attend opening events. For the *David Hammons: Hometown* exhibit, more than 800 attend. Usually, most of the people in attendance are white. At the Hammons opening, about 400 are African-American. For a racially polarized town like Springfield, Illinois, the mix is unusual and refreshing. I overhear someone say the turnout proves that the museum should invite more black artists. But I know the museum has invited many black artists. Never, in the history of the museum, has there been a party like this. This is Hammons country; he is loved.

It is hard to talk to David at the opening. Everyone wants to talk to him, wants him to autograph a book or T-shirt or program. He has hundreds of relatives and friends and all of them want to see him, talk to him. Especially one of his aunts, who, when he does not come to her quickly enough, drags him to her side by his ear.

The reception is catered by Boyd's: hot chicken wings, buttermilk and sweet potato pies, as well as cheese and fruit. Wine and beer are served, although David wanted stronger spirits. A jazz band plays. Two people tell me my jacket matches the wall.

And then it's over. We go to the top of the Hilton for a drink. Instead of the worker crowd, it's friends and family. I leave at 12:30. He presents a workshop the next morning for kids. I call him at 9 a.m. Sunday to tell him good-bye; he asks where I am going. He is still asleep. I tell him I am not going anywhere, but he is going to London. He says it's been wonderful.

Monday night, I have a psychic pop that jolts me out of bed at 2 a.m. A man is in my bedroom facing south, wearing a cap like David's and black leather jacket and pants. I can't see his face. I think he is real, but he de-materializes into a thousand mosaics — gray, black and orange. A friend says the experience was an apport. Usually he will leave something. I wish he had left my Japanese float; someone took it out of the pool.

I go to sell insurance. My client has a calendar on her table that says, "Rosemary is for remembrance."

Novel Excerpts

Walking Stories

I was born and raised in Springfield, Illinois. As I walk around my town, memories surface. Some are pleasant, and some are not so pleasant. I used to think I had control over what I remembered, but now I believe that, as Tennessee Williams once said, "Memory is seated predominantly in the heart." Walking Stories *is a collection of memories which have been compiled into a book of short stories. This short piece is one of the works included.*

As I walk around this city — my town, my hometown — every street seems to hold a house that holds a story. I remember, remember well, remember too well what happened to the people who once lived in a particular building, a certain apartment. I think of a friend from years ago. During her short stay in Springfield, she became involved with a doctor. He rented her an apartment — that's how she met him. After that, she found out about other things he did. The way he collected rent, for example, was through sexual favors. And the doctor, he was? He dispensed amphetamines. She was a mess when she left town.

The doctor was, in a roundabout way, an acquaintance of my uncle. My uncle told me stories about him once. It was a sunny afternoon in November 1979. I was in Encino visiting my aunt and uncle, who had invited me often to come out and see them. Usually I stayed in Illinois, where life was safe and secure — where my past, present and future were encased in a shroud, wrapped around me, now and forever. But this time, I had ventured out — moved to San Jose, California — the land of milk and honey, of vitamins and Calistoga.

I was not living the good life in California. I was on unemployment and I was smoking clove cigarettes, which my aunt thought were marijuana. They smelled funny, which was all she knew. My aunt was disgusted with me because I was not working. She thought I was disgraceful and I thought so too, so it wasn't a good time.

My uncle was nice to me. He was always nice to me, but on that particular day, he talked to me — something he hadn't done before. He told me stories about how when he was young, he had been a jazz musician. He gave it up when he married my aunt. She wouldn't have liked him hanging around bars, he said.

We were at the pool. I had always been very fond of my uncle. It was his smile, I think. The gleam in his eye. His gentle manner. And, although I had felt close to him, admired him, questioned his patience with my aunt, I had never talked to him.

I mentioned the doctor, the one I thought was a slime. I started out by testing my perceptions. "I know you are somewhat acquainted with Mort Rosen and his family in Springfield. He seems like such a sleaze. Is he a good doctor or is he a scumbag?"

"He's a sleaze," my uncle said immediately, without hesitation. "He's an evil man. That man. That family." Uncle threw up his hands. In his deep Clark Gable voice, he said, "Boy, did they get what they deserved. Such a story about that family I could tell you."

"Tell me," I said. And then I became silent, hoping he wouldn't back out, hoping he wouldn't do what he always did — find the good things to say. I waited quietly, patiently, for him to sort through his memories. I was excited. He had never told me a story before. I don't know that he had ever said anything in particular to me. I had always told him he looked like Clark Gable and he had smiled. He had the cutest mustache and he was a wonderful dancer. And terribly sweet. I could see it in every part of him — his eyes, his walk, his gestures, his tolerance, his patience with my aunt who nagged him and nagged him.

And now we sat together, at the pool, at the condo his millionaire son had given him. I dangled my feet in the water. He sat in a lawn chair, close to me.

"I palled around with them for a while, you know — with the Rosens." He nodded his head. "Yes, I did," he repeated as if to convince himself that the story he was about to tell did indeed happen a long time ago.

"My mother was their cleaning lady." He nodded. "My father left when I was born. I didn't know my father." A note of sadness clung in the air. "I don't even know how well she knew him." Did he say his mother had a lot of men? Or did he imply it? I can't remember. "Oh, what they did to make money," he said. It was almost a groan. "And the way they treated my mother.

"The Rosens owned a lot of businesses. They had a couple

houses, a tavern, a used furniture store and a retail store. All of this was on Washington Street you know — a couple blocks north of where you used to live. But a long time ago, when the miners were working in Springfield, they would cheat them. Oh, how they would cheat them. They would give them credit and charge them more for things. They cheated them blind."

Uncle had a look of distaste. He furrowed his brow, wrinkled his mouth.

"And they paid for it. For their cheating and their lying. All the pain they inflicted on other people — they got it back twofold. They paid for all of it. You can't do the things they did to people and not pay. It's a law of nature. What you do to other people you get done to you."

He paused.

He told me the Rosens had three children — Mort, Ira and Sadie. "Mort married a wonderful woman. I was fond of her. So was my mother. But Mort didn't appreciate her. She was, still is, a fine person. Her name was Lillian. And she was too good for him, that's for sure. He took so many mistresses — one he really wanted to marry. But Lillian would not give Mort a divorce. She wouldn't give him one. She knew that's what he wanted the most and she kept it from him. That was her main goal in life — to see that he could not have what he wanted most. Lillian was such a lady, he couldn't find any grounds to divorce her.

"Sadie married when she was very young. She married Morris Abraham, who had a tailor shop on Seventh Street. Sadie's mom and dad never liked Morris. They thought Sadie was too good for him. Nobody was good enough for them. Morris was a good man, a nice man. He didn't deserve that family, that's for sure. Sadie was the only one out of the family who was any good. It was like she didn't belong to them. She was beautiful and she was good. She was the light of her mother and dad's life. She was. They doted on her."

He told me about the day when they all went swimming out at the lake. "We had a picnic and then went swimming. Sadie didn't know how to swim. She waded out in the water. We were busy playing ball. After a while I realized that she wasn't around. I dived in the water and looked for her. She was dead. She was only 17. It was a tragedy.

"Ira was studying to be a dentist. He was going to school in St. Louis. He used to stop by and visit me and your aunt. We were living there then. He fell in love with a wonderful woman. She was lovely and oh, so sweet. She reminded me of Sadie, in a way. But Ira's parents had a fit. The mother set out to poison Ira against the girl. And she did, too. The girl tried to hold onto Ira, tried to tell him what his mother and father were doing. But eventually the mother got her way. Ira left her.

"He came home from St. Louis and married a woman from Springfield. She ran off with another man. He married again. The second wife got polio; she died. He married for a third time. This time he married a shiksa. The shiksa took another woman in. She was a lezzie. Ira supported both of them, just to keep it quiet. This wife killed herself after two years. She hung herself in the bedroom."

He shook his head.

"Yes, that family. They got back all the tragedy that they put on other people. It was a shame. There are some people who are just evil, I believe, and I think that was one evil family. With the exception of Sadie, who died early, they were all evil. My mother would scrub their floors and clean their houses and they would try to cheat her out of the little pittance they paid her. They would give her food to take home that wasn't fit for a dog to eat.

"They had a lot of money though. You know how they made their money? The Rosens? They manufactured stills during prohibition. Yes, they did.

"Your aunt is calling us now. It's time to eat. You could use a good meal. Let's go. Enough of them. Just thinking of that family makes me angry. The way they treated people. You can't do that. You have to get paid back for what you do. That's the law."

My aunt was waiting for me when I walked into the house. She had fixed braised brisket of beef and it was delicious.

"I hate to see you going out with a colored man."

"He's not colored," I said. "He's Mexican. Mexican-American."

"Aunt Evelyn said he was colored."

"He's not."

"Is that right? Why would she say that?"

"I don't know. I suppose he looked darker than anyone else at Mom's funeral."

"I don't want to see my niece with a colored man."

"He's not colored."

"I'm not prejudiced or anything, but you know what I mean."

"Yes."

"If I saw you walking down the street with a colored man holding your hand, it would make me sick."

"Yes, I understand."

"One of my best girlfriends was colored when I was in grade school. I'm not prejudiced."

"Yes, I understand."

"Do you? Do you really?"

The phone rang and I did not have to explain how I really did understand, which she wouldn't understand anyway.

I listened to her talk on the phone to her friends, tried to get a glimpse of her life. I was alone in the plush living room with the brocade sofas covered with plastic transparent cushions which protected them from visitors like me.

"Now, wait a minute," said my aunt on the phone. "Can I tell you how I'm feeling? You won't let me finish. Wait. You didn't let me finish. How old is your Hadassah?" The conversation went on and on. I got the idea my aunt had been instrumental in starting a new group. She was a newcomer to an old group and didn't like it. Now she had a new one. I thought about this. Her parting words on the phone were, "If Annette Rose goes, I'm not going."

She hung up. Packed a care package for my ride back home. "You've got to admire your sister," she said. "She takes care of herself. She doesn't ask anybody for anything."

I was silent. I told myself that someday I would work, would have a job, would find something someone would hire me to do. "I'll get a job soon," I said. "Maybe I'll get two."

"Ha," she said. "You'll never amount to anything. If you haven't amounted to anything yet, you never will. I worked ever since I was in the eighth grade. I sold peanuts at the fair. I bought a big bag for 25 cents and divided them into several bags. Sold them for a dime. A policeman kicked me out twice. My son was sick, but he went to work doubled over in pain. He wasn't a quitter."

In an attempt to redeem myself, I said, "Well, I'm a writer. I get lots of rejections but I keep writing. I don't think I'm a quitter."

"Maybe you are in the wrong field if you keep getting rejected," she said. "I took any kind of job I could get regardless of whether it was in my field or not. I never asked nobody for nothing. I don't know what's the matter with you. You are an intelligent girl. You must find other things more important than being successful — what, I don't know."

I left them at the door. Uncle followed me out, stuck a $10 bill in my shirt pocket when Aunt wasn't looking. He placed his index finger to his lips and said, "Shhhhhhh — don't tell her."

I walked away thinking how strange that he wasn't even my blood relative. It was she who was my mother's sister.

No Compromising Positions
(From *Fifth Position*)

It is a cold Midwestern January night. I stand in the doorway under the neon dancing figures — the old Arthur Murray Studio. I check the flyer posted in the glass case. It is cold and dark and I cannot read the flyer, so I go up the stairs to find out the offerings.

A sweet smell greets me as I enter the corridor leading upstairs. A smell like incense, mixed with other smells — an unusual smell. Large, lifelike African figures are painted on the beige walls. Large masks hang from the walls — *objets d'art*. A small green chalkboard hangs above the desk with a four-line message on it in white chalk. It is written like a poem in a language that I don't understand.

There is a desk and a chair and a woman sitting behind the desk to my left. To my right is a large heavy curtain. It is pulled across the opening so I cannot see into the space where the classes are being held.

"Can I help you?" the woman behind the desk asks.

"Yes. I'd like to take a jazz dance class," I answer.

"We don't have jazz dance. We have body conditioning tonight."

I am visibly disappointed.

"Would you like to sign up for body conditioning?" she asks in a plain tone, neither betraying friendliness nor unfriendliness.

"Oh no," I say. "I hate exercises."

"I don't think this will be what you expect," she says.

I think about it. The reason I hate exercises is because I am uncoordinated. I cannot touch my toes. I will be letting myself in for a big embarrassment. Oh well, I say to myself. What the hell. I have a leotard on already. I've faced part of the worst. I'm dressed. The kids have a sitter. My body can use it. Why not?

I pay my $2.50 and go into the dressing room.

After undressing (I wear my tights and leotard under my street clothes), I walk out into the studio — a long room with hardwood floors and mirrors and a barre which extends all around the room.

I stand limp in this beautiful space, not knowing what to do with myself. One glance in the mirror reflects a large fat white dowdy figure. I turn away. Who is the woman in the mirror? She looks about four months pregnant. Her hair is more brown than gray. Or more gray than brown? I do not look in the mirror again.

Women are jogging around the room. I am lost in a swirl of color while they whirl. Pastels fly by me — aqua, peach, pink, purple. Silk paisley scarves wave at me and bells are jingling — ankle adornments.

A man appears with two young men flanking him, carrying floor-size conga drums.

Everyone sits on the floor in their own space.

A majestic presence enters the room. I can feel it before I see it — a presence, a woman, something I have never felt before. The Teacher.

She faces the class smiling and greets everyone. She wears a peach-colored silk Capezio leotard with rust-colored tights, and a paisley silk scarf ties around her waist. Bright-colored Indian-designed pastel woolen leg warmers cover a portion of her legs from the lower thigh to right above the ankle.

"Lie flat on your backs, please," she says. "I want you to breathe in to the count of four and then exhale to the count of four. I will demonstrate. Breathe in ... two, three, four ... and out ... two, three, four."

The drums begin.

"Now we are ready to do the exercise. I want you to lift your right leg. Eight counts. And then your left. I want you to watch me first, and then you do it. Right leg ... one, two, three, four, five, six, seven, eight. Left leg ... speed it up ... two, three, four, five, six, seven, eight. Faster ... two three four five six seven eight."

Fall, flat back, fall, flat back.

Jumping jacks, 50, pliés, relevé, sit-ups, stretches and bounce, bounce, bounce.

I cannot do the exercises.

Next, dance progressions across the floor. Just a walk at first, across the floor, in threes. Walk with stomach in and head held high. Strut. Walk, two, three, four. Turn, two, three, four. Circle, two, three, four and walk, two, three, four.

The Teacher laughs because the students cannot get the simple steps correct. At least one of the three turns the wrong way. Many of us do not know our left from our right. The dance steps get considerably more difficult each time we go across the floor. The steps are very intricate.

The class lasts an hour and a half. Everyone is lying in their own respective pools of sweat. I have half-heartedly attempted all of the steps, but have done none of them right. Mostly I've just gaped at The Teacher, the peach-clad figure that performed the ritual.

"What's the matter with you, girl?" The Teacher asks after class. "You're looking at me like I'm not for real."

"It was wonderful," I say.

It sounds so trite. "You are so beautiful," I want to say. "So elegant and so magical."

I go back again and again, twice a week, for body conditioning, and sometimes three times a week.

The Teacher talks with us about how we look. "I don't allow my students to wear black in the classroom. I would like for you to order the proper attire."

I want to be pretty too, to be able to look in the mirror without cringing. I order a light aqua silk Capezio leotard with matching tights. I order a dance girdle to rid me of my pregnancy — although it is false, not real. At The Teacher's ominous suggestion, I put on a bra. I select old silk scarves out of my drawers at home — scarves that have a smattering of aqua in them — to decorate my costume. Color-coordinated, so to speak. I want my outfit to be just right, to be complete.

The transformation is not what I expect. I am still white.

I try putting on lipstick to give my face some color. The deep red is harsh against my pale, and the pink gives me a zombie-like look.

Regardless of my skin, my lack of color, I continue to perform in the ritual. I go twice a week to perform it. I am getting in shape.

The ritual is performed with reverence, but there is hostility too. I weigh each night before I go whether it is worth it. There is one woman in particular who does not have an affinity for palefaces. I call her Awning Eyes. Her eyelids droop; they are always half-shut. Her contacts, she says.

Once, when I am in the dressing room gyrating to the music — drummers, five of them in the small room next to the dressing room, pounding until the wall vibrates — a child says, to no one in particular while she watches me, "She's too fast."

"They all too fast," Awning Eyes answers.

Another time I smile at her, wanting friendliness.

"I hafta smile at y'all every day and I ain't doing it here."

I can never tell. Sometimes the ritual is mixed — two-thirds reverence, one-third hostility. It depends on who shows up. It is not rigidly structured. There are as few as 10 and as many as 30. When there are 30, I make myself invisible. There are 10 regulars — the dance troupe.

I am in love with The Teacher. I ask her if I can do an article on her school for the local newspaper. She eyes me suspiciously and says I can as long as she sees it before it is printed.

I figure she will never trust me. Why should she? Do I trust her?

I find out during the interview that The Teacher studied under Katherine Dunham and the method of dance she teaches is Dunham Technique — a combination of primitive, jazz, ballet and African. Dunham studied in Haiti. Dunham does not just teach dance in her school, but she has a total outlook, The Teacher says. The Whole Self.

It takes a long time for the article to appear in the newspaper. I write it in March and it is published in June.

I am unprepared for the celebrity status I have achieved upon publication. The next time I walk into the studio — as usual, timid, keeping my place — I am hugged by three women who are holding the paper and laughing and jumping up and down. They are thrilled to see their pictures in the paper. They are nice to me.

I want the women to accept me.

It is June and I go East for a vacation. I am out of town for two weeks. I return home. I stay away from class as long as I can, telling myself not to go somewhere I don't belong. I tell myself to forget it. Or, as my grandmother would have said, "Leave it be."

My body begins to throb, unconsciously.

I see someone on the street who says they have mail for me at the dance studio.

I go back.

Again, I am unprepared for the reception. The Teacher comes out and puts her arms around me.

"Girl," she says. "Don't you ever stay away so long. Where have you been?"

Another woman says, "Girl, look at you. You darker than I am."

"I work at it," I answer.

I am happy.

After class, the drummer is standing in the hallway by the dressing room. For the first time, I speak to him. "I really enjoyed the drums tonight. I've missed them."

"I hear ya," he says.

When I finish dressing and walk outside into the warm

summer night, he is leaning against the building.

"So you like the drums, huh?"

"Yes I do. I get stoned before I come to class and it feels like they are beating right inside my skull."

"You got any more?" he asks.

"More?" I repeat.

"More smoke?"

"I might have. I dunno." I begin rifling through my purse.

"Wanna go to my place and smoke it?" he asks.

I am wary.

"It's just right next door in the hotel," he says, pointing to the building next to the studio.

"Yeah. Sure. Why not?"

That is the beginning. We see each other for about eight months, on and off. The meetings are infrequent — short interludes at my place. The same ritual every time. The lights are off. We light a candle. He lights a joint. He puts on one record, *Soul Makossa* by Manu Dibango. All conga drums and African chants. Hypnotic. I tell him the record reminds me of him, of his music.

The experience is titillating, but not satisfying.

It is January 1978. He no longer comes to play drums at the class. Something is missing.

In February, my apartment is broken into and I accuse him of doing it.

"Man, this is 1978," he says.

A few months later, the studio closes and moves out of town.

He comes back a year later to say hello. I am involved with another man. We walk briefly into the downstairs of my apartment.

Two years later, I find out that the teenage boys down the street staged the break-in.

I am humiliated and embarrassed.

The pastel leotard hangs on a hook in the bathroom, unused. The offerings have been collected.

Excerpt from *Fifth Position*

He was waiting at the bar when I walked in. Sitting at the back of the bar. Short. Mexican. Glasses. Not thin. Not fat. I walked in feeling approximately 14 feet taller than him. Every time I looked at him, I wondered why I was attracted to him.

I ordered a Jack Daniels on the rocks and paid for it myself. I still couldn't get used to that. My generation didn't do things like that. That was supposed to be compensation for having a date — they paid.

"Table for two?" he asked, gesturing toward a small round table.

"Don't mind if I do," I said, eager to dig into my Jack Daniels.

We sat down at a table.

I had been sick for a week and had stopped smoking. My body didn't know what to do without abuse. Ballet class had ended for the month of August; jazz class too. I had no place to abuse my body/mind/soul.

The Jack Daniels I sipped tasted as good as I had anticipated. There was a little bit too much of it for me, but how was I to know?

While we were sitting at the table, another friend of his came and joined us. This particular man had a degree in English, as did we all (the Mex and I), and also had hair down to his feet. He'd let it grow for seven years. I knew that because some straight-looking man had stopped by the table and asked him how long he had to let it grow to get it that long. He had answered "seven years" and had looked embarrassed and flattered.

Right now I was looking at the Mexican and he was smiling.

His friend, the seven-year-hair man, yakked for a while about Hemingway. I knew this guy from school and he never talked about much else besides Hemingway. I often wondered if he knew anything else. The hair man spent much of his time trying to write like Hemingway.

Both boys compared where they had sent their stories and poems and discussed who'd been published where, ad nauseum, ad nauseum.

I began telling the boys about my great friend who had written this great novel.

Long Hair wanted to meet her.

Why did I do it?

"Go call her. Go call your friend," he half-ordered.

I hesitated.

Why, I thought? Why am I going to do this? Would she like him? Would he like her? Would I be sorry if they didn't like each other?

"Matchmaker, matchmaker, make me a match. Find me a find. Catch me a catch." (From *Fiddler on the Roof*.)

A true yenta would have charged for the service, but I was paying my dues for the game I had invented, or tried to play — one-up.

I got up and walked slowly, with my head up, to the pay phone at the end of the bar. I put my feet in Fifth Position and dialed the number.

Busy.

I walked back to the table. I was beginning to feel Jack. He had a hold of me and was making me a tiny bit woozy. When I sat down at the table, the Mexican told me he had been fasting. He said he was hungry.

Every time anybody said they were hungry in the past year, I would recite Emily Dickinson:

> I had been hungry all the years
> my noon had come to dine
> I trembling drew the table near
> And touched the curious wine ...

The poem produced vacant stares. Literature majors not familiar with Emily D. Tsk, tsk.

Long Hair was yapping about something. I was drunk. He was asking questions about my friend.

"What does she look like? How tall is she?"

"About as tall as he is," I said, pointing to the Mexican.

"Good. Ummm. Well, what does she look like?"

"She's just beautiful. She's brilliant. She has a musical voice. I mean, her voice rises and falls and you can almost see where she puts her commas in when she talks."

They stared, both of them — at me.

All of a sudden I had a sneaking feeling that women's standards of beauty might be different from men's. I verbalized my fear. I asked them to tell me a man they thought was beautiful.

"Burt Reynolds," said the Mexican. "Tony Quinn."

I agreed with Tony Quinn.

"Who?" asked Long Hair.

"Tony Quinn," said the Mex. "Zorba the Greek."

"Oh yeah," said Long Hair. "Zorba."

I loved the Mexican.

"Let's order a cheese plate," I said. "I'm starved and drunk. I haven't eaten since 10:30 a.m."

"I haven't eaten for two days," said the Mexican.

"Why not?" I asked. "You trying to lose weight?"

"Call your friend," Long Hair ordered.

I got up and walked, two major achievements considering my intake of Jack Daniels. I had to concentrate on how far I had to go, which was not far because the bar was small and narrow. At this point though, every step counted.

I dialed.

Busy.

Dimes in hand, I sat down.

"Order a cheese plate," said Long Hair to the Mex. "I'll pay half."

"Jesus," I said. "It's only 50 cents."

I felt like a bigmouth.

Long Hair placed the 50-cent order like he was ordering at Maxim's, then offhandedly said to us, "Cheddar and brick. Is that okay?"

I looked at the Mexican. The Mexican looked at me.

"No," I said. "Hot pepper."

"Hot pepper," said the Mexican at the same time. I had finally found someone who liked hot pepper cheese.

We ate, I drank, and Long Hair kept bugging me to call my friend.

I was feeling woozy.

I again made the long journey to the telephone. I dialed.

It rang.

"Hello," I said. "Is Sunny there?"

"Hello," said a very straight, formal voice. "I'm not sure. Who's calling?"

"This is Anna."

"Oh, Anna. How is your cold?"

"Fine, just fine."

"Really? Sunny said you were quite sick last night."

"Oh yeah, I was. I mean I still am. But I'm much better." The Jack Daniels helped. I no longer felt anything. I couldn't even remember that I'd had a cold last night. I was focusing on the sign outside the door window that said Southtown TV. I was bending over, flat-back, with one finger in my ear to shut out the sounds of the bar lest mama on the phone heard and thought I was a heathen. Fifth Position was shaky and wobbly.

"Sunny is gardening outside quite a ways from here. I'll try to get her. It might take her a while to come to the phone."

"Oh, that's okay. I can wait." As long as I could stand up. Fifth Position was gone. I was doubled over, leaning against the wall. The bowery twirl had replaced Fifth.

"Hello."

"Sunny. Hello. Hi. How are you?"

"I'm fine. How are you? Where are you?"

The emphasis when she spoke was on the where.

"I'm drunk. At a bar. With two friends. They want to meet you."

"Oh. My. Where are you?"

"At the Stopped Clock."

"Where is that?"

"South Street. South and something. I'm across from a bar, a TV repair place and a movie theater."

"Hmmmm. I don't think I know where that is. South and what?"

"Eleventh. Eleventh and South."

"Is that near the library?"

"Yeah, yeah, it's south of there."

"It can't be south."

"No, it's north. I mean east. It's east of there."

"Hmmm. I think I know where it is. I've been gardening though. It will take me a while to get ready."

"How long?" (I was worried about the hungry Mexican.)

"Thirty to 45 minutes."

"Okay."

"Is that okay? Will you still be there?"

"Yeah, I'll be here." I would be a puddle by then, a puddle of Jack Daniels on the floor of the bar. Kids would walk in me without their boots and their mothers would get mad. "Yeah, honey. I'll be here."

Back at the table, the Mexican was wearing a hungry look. For food, I thought at first. Then I realized it was for me.

"Are you hungry?" he asked.

"Oh yeah." I looked him up and down. "You betcha."

The Mexican was getting hotter. His insides glowed like neon.
"What are you hungry for?" he asked.
I leaned forward and whispered that I was hungry for someone to touch me and hold me and kiss me.
He was amused, intrigued, turned on and hot.
"Hummm," he said. "Let's go eat now."
"No. Can't. Friend coming. Got to stay," I said.
"How long?"
"Huh?"
"How long do we have to stay after your friend comes?"
"Don't know."
Jack had gotten the best of me. I was now sipping water.
The Mexican was pressuring me for answers I couldn't give him. Long Hair was uncomfortable because we were drinking each other in like parched-desert partners.
I felt the need to urinate.
"I hafta pee," I announced. Then I stood up.
"Gee," said Long Hair. "I hope I'm not holding you guys up. I shouldn't have told you to call her. I feel like I'm holding you two up."
"You are," I said. "You are holding us up from eating and dancing. But I will forgive you."
I stomped off to the john.
The Mexican smiled. Long Hair shook his head.
I peed.
When I staggered, flounced, relevéd, and pliéd my way back to the table, Sunny was there carrying on a conversation with the boys. She was talking in a voice somewhere between Ginger Rodgers and Mary Martin. She looked pretty with long chestnut hair and she was wearing aqua tones.
"This is Sunny, you guys."
"Yes," Sunny said. "I came in and they knew."
The Mexican wanted to know when we were going to eat.
"Anna tells us you are writing a novel," said Long Hair to Sunny.
"Yes," she said. "I've just finished."
"Really," said Long Hair, as if he thought she might be making it up.
"Yeah," I said, as I leaped into the opening in the conversation, pretending this was an interview. I started acting weird like interviewers. "Tell me, dahling, is it true that you've finished your first novel?"
"Yes, that's quite true," Sunny said.
"And, my deah, is it autobiographical?"

"Well," said Sunny. "Let's just say it's fiction."

"When are we going to eat?" asked the Mexican.

I leaned over to pacify him, but in my condition his proposition — my proposition (whose idea was it to get together anyway?) — was sounding better.

"Can't we just get up and leave?" he asked.

"No. No. No. No." I pleaded.

"How are we going to be alone together?"

"I don't know," I said.

We chattered and drank and Sunny and Long Hair talked and I finally said that the Mexican was hungry. We must go eat. We would all meet back at my house. I gave them the key. I was, by this time, totally incapacitated. I could not drive. I got in the car with the Mexican. He leaned over and kissed me. I moaned and licked his lips and teeth. He moaned. He kissed my hand. I moaned. He drove. I tried to lower my body chemistry by thinking about food instead of sex.

"What do you feel like eating?" he asked.

"Anything. Really. I hate decisions. You choose. I really don't care. I really don't."

"Well, I wanted catfish. But I'm thinking about fast food."

"Uh-huh."

Fast food and slow sex. I thought that, but didn't say it. All I could think about was guarding my passion, lest I appeared as desperate as I felt. Body chemistry was hitting a high 10, on a 1 to 10 scale.

We pulled into some fast-food facility and I ordered, believe it or not, baked beans. Not everybody ate hamburgers. He did.

We came home to my place.

Sunny was there listening to George Benson. I asked where Long Hair was.

"He had kidney problems," she said. "He had to leave."

I couldn't believe it. After all that yapping about wanting to meet her. Disappointment registered in my face. Sunny read it.

"He took my phone number though. I gave it to him on a deposit slip. Clever, don't you think? I used to hand out matchbooks."

Actually I had no desire to try it. I just didn't know what else to say.

"It's very effective."

I put on Lamber, Hendricks and Ross.

I lit a joint, then some incense. The three of us stood watching the turntable go around. I began to dance. Alone. Sunny and Fidel watched me. I stopped. I thought of how the two of them should be together instead of him and me. I was 40 heads taller than him.

Eventually, Sunny left.

I turned off the lights and began to dance with Fidel, slowly. Annie Ross sang softly in my ears. We swayed to mellow tunes murmured through the speakers. I felt the familiar numbness in my head.

The Mexican caressed me. I felt my blouse go over my head. He kissed me, licked my nipples. I moaned. We lay on the floor. My diaphragm was in, thank god. He licked my breasts, sucked my nipples in and out. He put his hand "down there" (Ella's euphemism) and moaned because it was so wet. I moaned because I saw his penis and it was huge. I stroked it, unsure whether it felt like silk or velvet. I wanted to ask him, but my contact with reality was tenuous; I was in and out of it. He sucked my lower lip gently, licked the inside of my knees and calves, licked my teeth and mouth.

He lay on his back. I planted small, wet kisses on his penis. He made animal sounds. I licked the upper side of the shaft. I could tell by the noises emanating from him, low and deep, that he was in ecstasy. I pretended his organ was mine. He smelled fresh, like LaFayette — no genital smell available to call up. Fresh silk or velvet. My mouth encompassed all of him. He cried out: pleasure. I hadn't bit him yet.

I put the drum record on the stereo.

I was at dance class. The drumbeats took me into the realm of consciousness where movement took over, where the mind stopped and the hypnotism began. I became the dancer, using Fidel as my space. I ate him to the rhythm of the drums, used my tongue to do a dance on him. My tongue became my feet. He had never been danced on before, I could tell. I had never danced on anyone — the penis-tongue dance.

I fantasized having the dance choreographed. I would wear a long pink velvet cylinder with black silk backing. I bounced up and down. It was easier and more fun than Fifth Position — more natural too. He tasted good. I did not force my tongue to dance. I sucked and licked and chomped and gnawed, but not too hard. When I was through, I buried my nose in his balls and kissed them gently. He was out of his mind with joy. I lay next to him. I was through.

He rose and lay on top of me. He entered me slowly.

Two moans filled the room as he filled me up.

"It belongs to me," I said.

"Oh yes, yes," he whispered.

"Don't take it out. Ever. Give it all to me. I want everything. Put your balls in me too."

He whimpered.

We gyrated to the music. Dance class routines helped. Forward, to the side and back and out, forward, back, in, out.

He went crazy.

I pointed my toes. I tightened all my muscles. Fidel felt me tighten. He was afraid he would not be able to remove his penis. He was afraid I would squeeze it off.

I comforted him.

"It will never come out," I said. "It belongs to me now."

GINNY LEE PHOTO

About the author

Rosemary Richmond was a Springfield fiction writer, poet and essayist whose work has been published in *Writers' Bar-B-Q*, the *Alchemist Review*, *Two Way Mirrors*, *XX Chromosome Chronicle*, Brainchild Writers of Springfield anthologies and *Illinois Times*. She received her bachelor's and master's degrees at Sangamon State University, where she also taught creative writing and women's studies courses. She performed in FirstNight Springfield arts festivals and in readings throughout Illinois. She was a Friends of Lincoln Library Writer of the Year and the recipient of an individual Artist's Advancement Award from the Springfield Area Arts Council. As co-producer of *Works in Progress*, a public access television program featuring regional writers, and as a founding member of Brainchild Writers of Springfield, Rosie nurtured and encouraged numerous writers and artists over the years. In her memory, Sangamon State University has established a Rosemary Richmond scholarship for female undergraduate students aspiring to be writers, and the Springfield Area Arts Council now offers the Rosie Richmond Artist Advancement Awards to local artists for specific projects.

To Rosie

The first time I remember focusing on Rosie was the summer of '76 at Sangamon State in Lit 480: Modern Poetry. It was T.S. Eliot, Rilke, and "William Buttereggs" as she said her young son Al would pronounce it. Nose in her book, wearing straw hat, blouse, floral skirt and sandals, poised and posh, she must have recently migrated from some section of San Francisco. Were you as studious in your poetry lesson as I was of you? ... No surface or medium. What could Picasso, Renoir, Monet have done?

What made me fall in love with her, though I didn't know it then? It was the day we gathered at the cafeteria for refreshments and reflections on the morning lecture. I cannot speak for the camaraderie, but I was surely hooked by her humorous tale of the uninvited (?) big fish that came to dinner in a wagon pulled by alley kids. Her timing and unassuming charm has kept me laughing inside and out.

I'll never forget our first "date," if that is the proper word. Didn't know drinking a few beers and praying could yield such results. I asked or wished for an angel and five minutes later I was giving Rosie (a.k.a. Angel, she told me later) a ride home. Don't know how I managed a kiss that evening. Perhaps I was hit by a meteor, a confluence of strawberry daiquiris, coincidental tunes from cross-time musicians, summer heat and nightclub cool. *Metanoia* comes from rose petals and kissing them primal joy incarnate: *satori*...

Ricardo M. Amézquita